ADULTING LIFE SKILLS - NAVIGATING FRESHMAN YEAR AND BEYOND - A 2-IN-1 GUIDE

ESSENTIAL SKILLS FOR COLLEGE AND EVERYDAY LIFE

ROSE LYONS

CONTENTS

COLLEGE BOUND

LIFE SKILLS 101:

COLLEGE BOUND

PRACTICAL APPROACHES TO NAVIGATING ROOMMATE CHALLENGES, MANAGING TIME, AND BALANCING ACADEMIC & SOCIAL LIFE - YOUR FIRST STEP TO COLLEGE SUCCESS

PAY IT FORWARD

A SHINING OPPORTUNITY TO HELP ANOTHER YOUNG ADULT LIKE YOU!

WANT TO HELP OTHERS?

Thanks for picking up "College Bound: Practical Approaches to Navigating Roommate Challenges, Managing Time, and Balancing Academic & Social Life." As you dive into this guide, we're excited for it to become your secret weapon in conquering college life.

If a chapter really speaks to you or totally clicks, why not share the love? Your review could be the insider info that another student needs. Whenever you're ready, drop us your thoughts – they mean a lot to us and your fellow students.

Cheers to having you on board. Eager to hear how you rock your college journey with these strategies!

Brooklyn,

From the very start, when I first cradled you, it was pretty clear you weren't your average kid – tons of energy, always curious, and never afraid to dive into things headfirst! You were like a little tornado, and keeping up with you was an adventure in itself, but one I wouldn't trade for anything.

Now, you've grown into this incredibly kind, happy, and downright goofy daughter, and that boundless energy of yours is still just as infectious. Thanks for being authentically you and never being afraid to be yourself. I couldn't be prouder of the amazing adult you're turning into.

As you step into your next big chapter, remember one thing: I'm your biggest fan. You're going to rock this world, and I can't wait to see all the awesome stuff you'll do. Here's to you and your never-ending supply of energy! And just so you know, there's absolutely nothing you could ever do to change how much I love you.

With all my love and endless support,

Mom

INTRODUCTION

Picture this: you're on the edge of something big, like really big. Can you feel the winds of change ruffling your hair? Okay, maybe that's a bit cheesy, but here's the deal: college life is about to unfold before you. It's more than just heavy textbooks, huge lecture halls, and those midnight ramen sessions.Whether it matches what you've seen in movies or heard from your older sibling, college is going to hit you differently. It's a major turning point, like a real metamorphosis. Seriously, it's that deep.

You're leaving behind the familiar hallways of high school and the cozy vibes of your hometown for a completely new and exciting adventure. How cool is that? But here's the thing, you're not alone in this. Your excitement, fears, hopes, and jitters? Trust me, tons of people feel the same way.

Meet Anna, this valedictorian with dreams as bright as a supernova. She steps onto campus, all ambitious and ready to conquer the world. But guess what? She quickly realizes that this place is a battleground of talent and brains, and her confidence takes a hit. Sound familiar? It's that moment we all go through when faced with sky-high expectations.

Then there's Ben, our resident gaming enthusiast, looking to find some peace in the college chaos. But guess what again? College is nothing like the serene haven he imagined. It's more like a whirlwind. Ever felt like your dreams clashed with reality? Ben sure has.

And don't forget Carlos, bursting with hope and dreams of engineering glory. But guess what one more time? Life hits him with budget woes, tight schedules, and language barriers. Still, he keeps on trucking. We've all been there when life takes a detour from our perfectly planned routes.

Now, you might be thinking, "I don't know these folks." Well, no duh! But their stories might just hit close to home once you're settling into college. You might find pieces of your own journey in their struggles and triumphs. You may know them after all.

But hey, let's get one thing straight. This book isn't here to scare you with tales of insurmountable obstacles. Nope. It's all about embracing the ups and downs, growing up, and dancing to the rhythm of gaining wisdom together with your college community. You got this!

I'm Rose Lyons, here to be your trusted companion on this

exhilarating journey. Unlike many self-help authors who offer the same tired advice, I aim to be more than just a writer; I want to be your friend and mentor throughout this book.

As you embark on the electrifying adventure of your freshman year, consider this book your beacon of guidance. Think of it as your support system, ready to assist you in navigating the challenges that are bound to come your way. This isn't just a collection of pages; it's your road map through the uncharted territory of college life, a valuable resource to help you tackle the hurdles that lie ahead. And always remember, your victories are not a matter of 'if,' but 'when.' You've got the potential for greatness!

1 INTO THE UNKNOWN

The only true wisdom is in knowing you know nothing. –Socrates

You might be surprised that a staggering 64% of college students are leaving their college education (31 Alarming College Students, 2022). And here's the kicker – it's not because they can't handle the academic or financial aspects. Nope, the real challenge often lies in the emotional and mental toll that college can take. Let's take a closer look at this hidden issue that's affecting campuses everywhere, casting a shadow on the future dreams and aspirations of tomorrow's leaders.

Close your eyes for a moment and envision once-vibrant university hallways, once buzzing with energy, now resonating with the silent echoes of despair. Young, hopeful minds fresh out of high school step into these corridors with dreams as diverse and radiant as autumn leaves swaying outside. They see college as the golden ticket to a promising future. Little do they know, beneath this shimmering facade lies a landscape of emotional turbulence and mental burdens, turning the college experience into an intricate obstacle course that many find too challenging to navigate.

The unspoken, ever-present specter of academic rigor in college often preys on students' peace of mind. It's akin to an ongoing academic Olympics, where everyone is vying for success in their chosen fields. However, the real challenge often lies beyond the academic load – it's the concealed emotional strain that lurks in the background. This strain encompasses stress, fear of inadequacy, and the anxiety of unmet expectations. These mental adversaries can erode a student's resilience, sometimes more significantly than the academic challenges themselves.

To counteract this, mastering time management becomes crucial. Learning to effectively manage time not only aids in coping with academic demands but also in balancing social life. Effective time management techniques can help mitigate stress and bolster academic success.

In addition to academic pressures, many students grapple with isolation in college. Transitioning from familiar environments to new settings can be daunting and may lead to feelings of alienation, which exacerbates stress and anxiety. Learning to balance social interactions and forge meaningful connections can provide a buffer against this isolation.

Financial pressures compound these challenges. The burden of tuition, housing, and living expenses weighs heavily, leading many to juggle part-time work with their studies. This balancing act can be draining, both mentally and emotionally.

Unfortunately, many college campuses lack sufficient mental health resources to support students through these multifaceted challenges. This chapter seeks to illuminate these issues, exploring their manifestations, consequences, and strategies for overcoming them. It emphasizes the importance of developing skills in time management, social engagement, and personal care as essential tools for navigating the complex terrain of college life

The Truth Will Set You Up for Success

Undoubtedly, it's a breeze to get caught up in the wave of rumors and partial truths that create a somewhat skewed image of what college life holds in store. And it's not inaccurate to say that your college journey will likely encompass these quintessential aspects. However, it's also important to acknowledge that the real college scene comprises elements that may not conform to the typical stereotypes.

So, rest assured, you haven't been fed a pack of lies. But here's the scoop – there's more to the college experience than meets the eye.

Myth 1: College Equals Endless Parties

Truth: While movies like "Animal House" and "Revenge of the Nerds" may make it seem like college is one never-ending party, the reality is quite different. Yes, there are parties, and yes, they can be memorable, but they're just one part of the college experience. For every wild night out, countless nights are spent studying, preparing for exams, and working on assignments. The allure of a non-stop party life needs to be balanced with the sobering truth of academic responsibilities.

Myth 2: The "Perfect" College Ensures Success

Truth: The idea that attending an Ivy League or top-tier college guarantees a perfect life is a common misconception. Where you go to college influences your education but doesn't determine your success. Your achievements depend on the effort you put into your studies, the real-world experiences you gain, the skills you develop, and perhaps a little luck.

Myth 3: Your Chosen Major Dictates Your Career

Truth: Your choice of major doesn't lock you into a specific career path. Many professionals find success in fields unrelated to their major. While your major equips you with a particular skill set and knowledge, it doesn't confine you to a single career track. Flexibility and adaptability often play a significant role in career development.

Myth 4: College Days Are the Pinnacle of Your Life

Truth: College can be a memorable and formative period in your life, as reflected in pop culture. However, the notion that these years are the absolute best of your life may limit your outlook on the adventures that await post-university. Life comprises various stages, each offering its unique and exciting experiences. You've already graduated from many life phases, and college is just one of them.

Myth 5: Professors Are Indifferent to Their Students

Truth: Despite their busy schedules and numerous students to attend to, most professors are not emotionless or detached. They are not the academic version of Voldemort or dementors. In reality, many professors genuinely care about their students' success and are willing to offer assistance when needed. Building relationships with professors can be a valuable part of your college experience.

Myth 6: You Need to Have Your Entire Life Figured Out

Truth: It's okay not to have your entire life mapped out when you start college. Most students enter college with varying degrees of uncertainty about their future careers and life paths. College is a time to explore, discover new interests, and clarify your goals. You have the flexibility to change majors or career plans as you learn and grow.

Myth 7: Everyone Else Has It All Together

Truth: It may seem like everyone around you has their life perfectly organized, but appearances can be deceiving. Many college students face challenges, doubts, and uncertainties like you do. Don't be too hard on yourself if you don't have everything figured out; you're not alone in your journey.

Myth 8: College is Only About Academics

Truth: While academics are a significant part of college, it's not the whole story. College offers many opportunities beyond the classroom, such as extracurricular activities, internships, networking events, and personal growth experiences. These non-academic experiences can be just as valuable in shaping your future.

Myth 9: You Must Excel in Every Aspect of College Life

Truth: Striving for excellence is admirable, but it's essential to remember that you don't have to be perfect in every aspect of college life. It's okay to experience setbacks, make mistakes, and ask for help when needed. College is as much about personal growth as it is about achieving high grades.

Myth 10: You Should Compare Your College Experience to Others

Truth: Comparing your college journey to others' can lead to unnecessary stress and feelings of inadequacy. Each person's path is unique, and what works for someone else may not be right for you. Focus on your goals, interests, and progress, and don't worry too much about how your experience measures up to others.

Myth 11: College Professors Always Have the Answers

Truth: Contrary to the belief that professors possess an answer to every question, they, too, encounter uncertainty in their fields. College is a place of exploration and inquiry, and professors often engage in ongoing research and learning to stay current in their areas of expertise. It's okay to challenge their ideas and engage in academic discussions.

Myth 12: You Must Stick to a Strict Major-Related Career Path

Truth: While aligning your major with your interests is essential, don't feel confined to a single career trajectory directly related to your field of study. Many successful professionals switch careers or explore diverse opportunities unrelated to their major. College provides a chance to develop various skills that can be applied in multiple contexts.

Myth 13: Professors Only Care About Grades

Truth: While grades are a part of academic evaluation, many professors genuinely care about your learning and growth. They value your class engagement, discussion participation, and willingness to seek help. Building relationships with professors can lead to mentorship and valuable career guidance.

Myth 14: You Must Graduate in Four Years or Less

Truth: The idea that college must be completed in exactly four years is a misconception. Many students take longer to graduate for various reasons, such as pursuing internships, working part-time, or changing majors. What's important is that you make the most of your college experience and graduate at your own pace.

Myth 15: College is Strictly About Individual Achievement

Truth: While personal growth and academic achievement are essential aspects of college, collaboration and teamwork are equally valuable. College provides opportunities to collaborate on projects, join clubs, and engage in group activities. These experiences enhance your interpersonal skills and contribute to your personal and professional development.

Key Takeaways:

As you start your college journey, remember that myths and truths are like two sides of the same coin. Navigating through the misconceptions about college with a clear understanding of reality is crucial. While college is a time of excitement and self-discovery, it's not always the picture-perfect experience that myths may suggest.

Now that we've debunked some common myths, you're better equipped to face the next section, where we'll explore what college feels like at first. Brace yourself for a rollercoaster ride of emotions, new beginnings, and unexpected discoveries as you step into this transformative phase of your life.

What Does It Feel Like at First?

Introducing Davis, a young and spirited individual who was tangled in a web of emotions as he packed his bags for the grand adventure of university life. His heart raced with a mix of anxiety and anticipation, questioning what lay ahead. Could he handle the distance from home? What about his old friends? And what kind of friends would he make here? The uncertainty was scary, but it was also undeniably exciting.

With a heartfelt farewell to his family and the familiarity of home, he hit the road toward the unknown. Doubts occasionally tugged at his determination, but his car wheels kept turning, taking him closer to his future.

When he arrived at the university, it loomed before him, a place steeped in tradition yet brimming with innovation. Even the air felt different here, carrying a sense of new beginnings. Those online conversations with his roommates had built up certain expectations, but meeting them in person was a bit of a reality check. They were different but also newbies like him, all seeking their place in this unfamiliar environment. His dorm room, once so strange and foreign, made him yearn for the comforts of home.

But soon after, following an outing with his roommates, he started to feel the sparks of excitement and independence that helped thaw his homesickness. Even as his accent became the subject of friendly jokes, he laughed along. Each day brought more introductions and fresh faces, making the experience feel thrilling and surreal.

Yet, that initial thrill gradually gave way to fatigue as time passed. During his first week, the excitement was replaced by the grind of daily routines. He even fell prey to the infamous "freshers' flu." But amid the coughs and sneezes of his fellow students, he found solace.

Davis's early days in college blended his expectations and reality. Looking back, his initial worries seemed somewhat comical. He had indeed plunged into a river of unknowns, but instead of being overwhelmed, he learned to adapt. Davis was now a university student, ready to embrace the ebb and flow of the college experience.

What Is College Like?

Imagine this: your first day, surrounded by an awe-inspiring display of diversity. Think of it as a vibrant mosaic, a tapestry woven from countless unique tiles representing different cultures, backgrounds, beliefs, and personalities. Each tile has its own story to tell, and when woven together, it creates a beautiful pattern of shared experiences and diverse perspectives. This, my friend, is the essence of college.

One of your early challenges will be learning to live independently. Depending on your perspective, you might be excited about answering only to yourself. However, consider that living relatively untethered, away from the guidance of your guardians, is akin to surviving in the wild: you have the freedom to enjoy the beauty of nature, but you also need to build your own shelter. From handling laundry to managing your budget, you'll become a master of various life skills. You'll establish your own routines, learn to respect others, and even become adept at settling disputes over the last slice of pizza.

Many college nights will be serene, with only the rustling of leaves or the soft tapping of keyboards to disturb the quiet. These peaceful moments often open the door to introspection, where you'll contemplate your path, progress, or even the latest plot twist in your favorite TV series. In college, balance is key. You'll discover when to relish solitude and when to embrace the company of others.

Then there's the ever-present companion of college life: stress. It may rear its head during late-night study sessions racing against deadlines, or trying to juggle your social life. But within that stress, and sometimes because of it, you'll tap into the resilience of your spirit. You'll develop ingenious time-management skills, learn to prioritize, and, most importantly, mature enough to seek help when needed. This leads us to self-discovery. College offers you the time and space to chisel out your self-portrait, uncovering your passions, strengths, and limitations, and, in the process, getting to know yourself in ways you've never imagined.

The truth about college is that it's a dynamic, unscripted, and enriching journey. It's not merely a stepping stone to a degree; you'll experience a symphony of victories, challenges, laughter, and learning, all interwoven with a healthy dose of chaos. It's the space where you evolve from an eager freshman into a confident graduate armed with a sharp mind, a broader perspective, and a profound understanding of yourself. Welcome to the adventure.

Fail Proof Yourself

A small-town boy, Alex, sets off on his college adventure, a mix of excitement and nervousness swirling in his stomach. His hometown, where everyone knows everyone, and life ambles at a leisurely pace, feels worlds apart from the bustling university campus. In a dorm room shared with city-slicker roommates who seem to have life figured out, discussing concepts he's never heard of and jetting off to places he's never dreamed of visiting.

College classes hit him harder than anticipated. The whirl-wind of fast-paced lectures and intricate subjects leaves him grappling to keep up. The library becomes his haven, an escape from the constant feeling of being out of his depth. He tries to fit in, joining study groups in the hope of making friends and grasping his coursework better, but often finds himself overshadowed by his more outspoken peers.

Financial pressures exacerbate his stress. While his scholar-ship covers part of his tuition, the rest is a relentless source of anxiety. He takes on a part-time job at a local café, serving coffee to students who chatter animatedly about upcoming adventures and sought-after internships. Every shift is a stark reminder of the wider world he yearns to explore.

Navigating the social scene at college becomes an enigma he can't quite solve. Invitations to parties and gatherings come his way, but he often declines due to work commitments or the gnawing fear of not fitting in. When he does attend, he feels like a silent observer, watching others effortlessly navigate this unfamiliar terrain.

As weeks blend into months, the mounting pressure starts to weigh him down. He keeps up a facade for his parents over the phone, trying to sound upbeat, but they sense the underlying distress. One fateful night, after a particularly grueling exam, he reaches his breaking point. Doubt seizes him, questioning if college is truly his path and if he's built for this life. His thoughts turn to his family and the sacrifices they've made, wondering if he's letting them down.

Eventually, Alex makes the agonizing decision to leave college. Returning home, he carries a mix of relief and disappointment. His parents, though supportive, hold concerns about his future. Back in his hometown, he reconnects with old friends and lands a job at a local hardware store. It's here that he begins to realize the value of the skills he picked up in college—time management, resilience, and self-sufficiency —all of which prove immensely beneficial beyond the classroom.

Determined to continue his education, Alex opts for online courses, forging his own path at a pace that suits him. In this new chapter of life, he finds fulfillment in the delicate balance of work, study, and living in the comforting embrace of his familiar surroundings. However, as he delves deeper into his online studies, he begins to yearn for the vibrant atmosphere of a college campus.

Alex comes to realize that he wants to return to college, armed with newfound wisdom and a better understanding of himself. With a more balanced approach to life and a renewed sense of purpose, he feels mentally prepared to embrace the challenges and opportunities that await him on a college campus once more. This decision marks a pivotal moment in his journey, demonstrating the resilience of the human spirit and the capacity for growth and change.

Set Yourself Up for Success

Let's delve into the mental aspect, where college life can resemble a seesaw, swinging between exhilarating highs and unsettling lows. It's perfectly normal to feel overwhelmed at times, but what sets you apart is the strength of your mental state. Nurturing a growth mindset that welcomes challenges, embraces the effort required for mastery, learns from feedback, and draws inspiration from the successes of others can keep you afloat, even in the choppiest of waters.

Success in college transcends merely securing top grades. While your GPA is one measure of success, true education encompasses more. Graduating with emotional intelligence, nurturing symbiotic relationships, and expanding self-awareness are vital facets of your journey. This entails recognizing and effectively managing your emotions and using them to guide your thoughts and actions. As mentioned, college offers a delightful mix of diverse cultures, perspectives, and ideas, which can open your mind and draw wisdom from every corner.

Mastering time management is another key to your triumph. If you decide to immerse yourself in college life fully, you'll contend with lectures, assignments, exams, social events, and extracurricular activities. However, if you invest in time management skills, you can meet your academic responsibilities while carving out space for leisure and relaxation.

Many college students face challenges because they lack a robust support network. College can sometimes feel isolating, and if you're naturally introverted, you might find it challenging to connect with others. It's crucial to forge bonds with your peers, engage in clubs and events, and be unafraid to seek help.

However, the most critical strategy of all is developing a self-care routine. Your journey through academia may become arduous if you neglect healthy eating, adequate sleep, and necessary breaks. Prioritizing your mental well-being is equally essential. Consider incorporating exercise to reduce stress, elevate mood, and sharpen cognitive abilities. Explore yoga, meditation, or any activity that quiets your mind and enhances focus.

While it would be lovely if success in college could be achieved effortlessly, the reality is that it demands a specific set of skills. Mental resilience, emotional maturity, adaptability, effective time management, strong support systems, and self-care are all integral components. Remember that every challenge on your path is also an opportunity to grow stronger and wiser. Heroes are not forged by comfort and ease; your resilience in the face of adversity is what shapes your character.

The Good, the Bad, and the Ugly

Embracing Dawn: Zion's Morning Marvel

Zion's story at Evergreen University isn't just about classes; it's about finding a rhythm in the chaos of college life. He navigates late-night study sessions, roomie jamming, and lazy afternoons in the quad, where frisbees fly and laughter echoes. His weekends are a mosaic of dorm movie nights and exploring the city's hidden gems with Craig.

Aria's freshman year at Rookfield Institute is a vibrant journey of self-discovery outside the classroom. She dives into cultural festivals, exploring new cuisines with friends, and finds solace in quiet coffee shop corners, journaling her thoughts. The art club becomes her sanctuary, where she paints and connects with fellow artists, while spontaneous road trips and star-gazing nights fill her with a sense of wonder and belonging.

While the ultimate goal of your college journey is to attain that coveted degree or diploma, there's so much more to explore along the way. Let's dive into the strategies that can help you build a solid foundation for your academic success.

Key Takeaways

- **College Life Is Full of Surprises:** College freshmen should be prepared for the unexpected. Like Aria, embrace the unpredictability and find joy in the twists and turns of your journey.
- **Diverse Connections Enrich the Experience:** Embrace connecting with people from diverse backgrounds. When you open up to cultural interactions, lifelong friendships and a broader perspective await.
- **Self-Discovery Is Part of the Process:** College is not just about academic achievements. It's a transformative journey that allows you to explore new passions, like Aria's love for painting, and discover more about yourself.
- **Balancing Academics and Campus Life:** Finding a balance between your studies and involvement in campus life, whether it's clubs, festivals, or other activities, is essential for a well-rounded college experience.
- **Setting a Solid Academic Foundation:** While college offers myriad experiences, don't forget the primary goal: earning your degree. In the next chapter, we'll explore strategies to ensure academic success.

2 WHY SOME FAIL

You're Not in Kansas Anymore: Why Some College Students Struggle Academically?

In the small town of Kansas, Emily, a young girl with notable academic talents, yearned for more than her familiar, comfortable life. Excelling in every school competition, she dreamt of broader horizons. When she got the chance to attend a prestigious East Coast college, she embraced it eagerly, though not without apprehension about the unknown challenges ahead.

At college, Emily encountered a level of competition and academic rigor she hadn't anticipated. Surrounded by peers as talented as herself and faced with demanding professors, she initially struggled, feeling out of place and questioning her abilities. However, Emily's resilience and determination drove her to seek help, join study groups, and dive deeper into her studies. This proactive approach led to a remarkable academic transformation.

By graduation, Emily had evolved from a small-town prodigy to a confident, accomplished scholar. Her success, reflected in her grades and the respect from her professors and peers, was a testament to her hard work and perseverance. Standing on the graduation stage, Emily realized her achievements were not despite her struggles but because of them. She had proven that success wasn't limited to her small-town origins but was attainable anywhere with persistence and adaptability.

Emily's story highlights the importance of embracing challenges, being open to growth, and the transformative power of perseverance in the face of adversity. Her journey from Kansas to college graduation symbolizes the journey of self-discovery and personal development many students undergo in their academic pursuits.

Why Are You Here? Let's Define Your Purpose

When pondering "Why am I in college?" the initial thought might be earning a degree for career advancement. But college offers more—endless possibilities, sharpening intellect, fostering curiosity, and preparing you for life's unpredictable journey. If your passion for a subject fuels your college path, it's a strong motivator, enhancing creativity and focus. Yet, passion should be balanced with practical, evolving goals. Set SMART goals, maintain a realistic balance in aspirations, and approach big dreams incrementally. College isn't just about a degree; it's a journey of personal growth and a stepping stone to achieving larger life goals. Each challenge you overcome builds resilience, bringing you closer to your ultimate objectives.

Strategies for Setting Effective College Goals

Craft SMART Goals: Define your goals precisely, ensuring they are Specific, Measurable, Achievable, Relevant, and Time-bound. For example, aim for an 'A' in a specific class, like biology, rather than a general desire to excel in the subject.

Maintain a Rhythmic Balance: Set high but realistic aspirations. Balance your academic ambitions with personal well-being to ensure a holistic approach to your college experience.

Dream Big, Act Incrementally: Visualize your ultimate dreams, such as making groundbreaking discoveries or writing a bestseller. Remember, these grand goals are achieved step by step. Start with smaller, achievable objectives that gradually build toward your larger dreams.

Develop Essential Life Skills: College is an ideal place to acquire life skills that will serve you well beyond graduation. Focus on developing skills like time management, critical thinking, teamwork, and effective communication. These skills are pivotal for academic success and crucial in your personal and professional life post-graduation.

Develop Critical Thinking Skills

In a world inundated with information, merely absorbing facts isn't enough. We must cultivate the art of critical thinking—the ability to extract meaning from data in a thoughtful, unbiased, and coherent manner. This cognitive toolkit isn't the exclusive domain of scholars or scientists; it's an essential set of skills for everyone, applicable in myriad contexts, from career choices to civic engagement and daily problem-solving.

So, what does this toolbox of critical thinking entail?

Imagine critical thinking as a collection of mental abilities that empower us to decipher the world around us. The University of Edinburgh defines these skills as the capacity to "identify, scrutinize, and assess arguments and evidence." Let's break down these capabilities:

Observation: This skill involves being keenly aware of your surroundings—identifying patterns, detecting changes, and noticing details others might miss.

Analysis: Think of this as your mental toolkit for unraveling information. It lets you dissect information, discern relationships, causes, and effects, and gain deeper insights.

Evaluation: This skill allows you to appraise the reliability of the information at your disposal. It's the tool you wield to determine the credibility and worth of information, arguments, or options.

Synthesis: You synthesize the information gathered at this stage, creating a fresh understanding or proposing solutions.

Communication: This involves the ability to express your thoughts in a clear, compelling manner.

How Do You Cultivate Critical Thinking?

Self-Assess Your Decision-Making Process: Dedicate time in your daily routine to review your decisions. Reflect on what you aimed to achieve, the options you considered, the pros and cons of each choice, the information that guided your decision, and the assumptions that influenced it.

Expand Your Perspective: Challenge yourself to see things from different viewpoints. Consider the motives, aspirations, and challenges of others, and engage with individuals who hold diverse experiences and opinions.

Practice Active Listening: Enhance your critical thinking by paying close attention to what others communicate. Show interest and respect through your words and body language, allowing you to understand their message, ask pertinent questions, and provide constructive feedback.

Break Down Your Information: Strive to comprehend the main points, arguments, or evidence in the information you're analyzing. This helps you understand the information's structure, logic, and validity and identify gaps, inconsistencies, or errors in reasoning.

Engage in Research: Seek out and collect relevant information from various sources to broaden your knowledge, challenge your views, and evaluate different information sources.

Nourish Your Curiosity: Cultivate an eagerness to learn and explore new things. Seek fresh information, ask questions, challenge assumptions, and uncover new connections.

Why Critical Thinking Matters

Critical thinking holds a unique allure, doesn't it? Let's peel back the layers and delve into its significance.

Embracing critical thinking encourages you to move beyond accepting facts at face value. Instead, you scrutinize and dissect them, gaining insight into the "how" and "why" of things. This process shapes your perspectives, encourages you to question the status quo, and reveals the myriad shades of life's complexities. Thanks to critical thinking, learning becomes a rich tapestry of wisdom where every morsel enlightens you.

But critical thinking doesn't merely enhance your intelligence; it also nurtures creativity and innovation. It prompts you to venture into uncharted territories, challenge conventions, and unveil innovative solutions. With critical thinking, you're not just a problem solver but also equipped to adapt and thrive in uncertainty. It sharpens your creative faculties, breathing life into your ability to think outside the box.

Critical Thinking in Every Aspect of Life

The essence of critical thinking extends far beyond the classroom. It plays a pivotal role in every facet of life, guiding decision-making and problem-solving. Here are some examples of how critical thinking manifests in various life domains:

College Life: Critical thinking empowers you to assess the reliability of information sources for research papers, dissect complex concepts, and engage in thought-provoking discussions with peers and professors.

First Jobs: In your career, critical thinking aids in problem-solving, decision-making, and innovation. It enables you to evaluate job opportunities, navigate challenges, and contribute fresh ideas to your organization.

Parenting: As a parent, critical thinking helps you make informed choices about your child's education, health, and well-being. It guides you in evaluating parenting advice, making decisions in your family's best interest, and fostering your child's intellectual development.

Travel: When exploring new places, critical thinking assists in planning itineraries, evaluating travel recommendations, and adapting to unexpected situations. It enhances your ability to immerse yourself in local cultures and make the most of your travel experiences.

Financial Planning: In managing finances, critical thinking enables you to analyze investment opportunities, make informed decisions about saving and spending, and plan for long-term financial goals.

Social Interactions: Understanding and empathizing with others, navigating social dynamics, and resolving conflicts.

Media Consumption: Discerning credible sources, understanding biases, and forming independent opinions.

Global Awareness: Interpreting world events, understanding cultural differences, and engaging in civic activities.

Critical thinking is the compass that guides you through life's complex terrain, enriching your experiences, enhancing your problem-solving abilities, and fostering continuous learning and growth.

Time Management and Blocking

The 50-30-20 Formula

Navigating the intricate dance of life, with its multiple dimensions like academics, work, social ties, and personal growth, can often feel like a high-wire act. But fear not; there's a method to bring order to this seeming chaos. Allow me to introduce the 50-30-20 formula, a clever strategy to harmonize your daily pursuits.

Imagine your workday as a delectable pie, divided into three mouthwatering slices. The largest portion, 50%, is reserved for nurturing your long-term aspirations. This is where you invest in your dreams, be it personal development, career planning, or academic endeavors. For instance, if you're charting a course toward becoming a lawyer, half of your day can be dedicated to law studies, online courses, or the pursuit of internships.

The next slice, accounting for 30% of your day, is aimed at mid-term goals, those tasks with looming deadlines in the coming months or years. While they may not directly align with your long-term vision, they serve as stepping stones toward it. If law is your calling, this portion of your day might involve completing assignments, preparing for exams, or networking with future colleagues.

The smallest slice, at 20%, caters to your immediate needs and daily responsibilities. Though they may appear mundane, these tasks are the nuts and bolts of your everyday life. So, if your goal is to grace the courtrooms one day, this fraction of your day could entail checking emails, answering phone calls, or tidying up your study space.

In the grand finale, remember this: The 50-30-20 formula serves as your compass, dividing your time into three harmonious parts—devotion to the future you aspire to (50%), the stepping stones toward it (30%), and the essential tasks of today (20%). Armed with this toolkit, you're well-equipped to orchestrate your life, find balance, and embark confidently on the path to your dreams.

Time Blocking Template

The 50-30-20 formula mentioned earlier could be applied within a time-blocking framework. Here's a table that you can use as a Time Blocking Template tailored to the 50-30-20 rule.

Time Slot	Task Type	Specific Activity	Notes/Goals
8:00 - 12:00	Long-Term Goals (50%)	Studying law-related subjects, taking online courses, etc.	
		Focus on career planning and personal development.	
12:00 - 1:00	Lunch Break		
1:00 - 5:00	Mid-Term Goals (30%)	Completing assignments, preparing for exams, etc.	
		Work on tasks with deadlines within a few months	
5:00 - 5:30	Break/Rest		
5:30 - 7:00	Immediate Goals (20%)	Check emails, return calls, household chores, etc.	
		Daily necessities, short-term tasks	
7:00 - 8:00	Dinner		
8:00 - 10:00	Personal Time	Hobbies, relaxation, etc.	

Please adjust the time slots and specific activities to suit your needs and priorities. You can also expand or contract the different sections based on the time you need for long-term, mid-term, and immediate goals. This table provides a structured way to visualize and organize your day, helping you stay focused and efficient.

As you step into the world of independence, a fresh chapter begins, bringing the need to reshape your family relationships. As you transition to college, discover the ways you can cultivate these connections, ensuring they continue to flourish and support you in this exciting new phase of your life. Keep reading to uncover the art of balancing family bonds as you embark on your academic adventure.

Mastering the art of time organization is potent in your collegiate toolkit, steering you toward achieving personal and academic aspirations. Balancing academic demands, social commitments, distractions, and the allure of procrastination can feel like a Herculean task. In this section, we'll explore the world of effective time management and introduce you to "hour structuring," which can empower you to craft and utilize your time precisely.

Unlocking the Benefits of Time Mastery

Mastery of time offers a range of rewards:

Enhanced Academic Success: Proficient time management skills can be your secret weapon, helping you meet deadlines, prepare for assessments, and avoid last-minute panic. This often results in improved grades and a deeper grasp of knowledge.

Stress Reduction: Effective time organization enables you to sidestep the last-minute rush and anxiety, allowing you to handle deadlines and expectations gracefully. This can translate into reduced stress and a greater sense of accomplishment.

Increased Productivity: Time mastery lets you accomplish more in less time. You can focus on the most critical tasks while minimizing disruptions and distractions, enhancing efficiency and work quality.

Improved Well-being: Effective time management maintains a healthy balance between academic responsibilities and personal life, ensuring ample time for health, hobbies, relationships, and leisure. This contributes to better physical, mental, and emotional well-being.

Structuring Your Hours—A Technique for Time Mastery

Structuring your hours involves dividing your day into blocks of time, each dedicated to a specific task or activity. The concept is built on the idea that planning and organization of your hours can fine-tune your focus, drive, and productivity. While this technique can be customized to your unique needs and goals, here's a general outline to guide you:

Focus on Goals: Identify your short-term and long-term academic and personal goals. Be specific and express them clearly.

Goal Breakdown: Divide your goals into manageable, bite-sized tasks or steps needed for achievement.

Time Estimation: Estimate the time required for each task realistically, considering your abilities, resources, and constraints. Timing your tasks can be helpful in this process.

Create a Schedule: Develop a schedule or calendar that assigns each task to a specific time block. Include your classes, work hours, meals, breaks, and other commitments in your schedule.

Stick to the Schedule: Make an effort to adhere to your schedule, focusing on the task at hand until completion or the end of the time block.

Schedule Review: Evaluate your schedule at the end of each day or week, identifying strengths and areas for improvement.

Tips for Effective Time Block Utilization

As you structure your hours in college, consider these tips:

Flexibility: Adjust your schedule when necessary, allowing for unexpected changes and emergencies.

Realism: Avoid overloading every moment with tasks. Allocate buffer time for transitions or unforeseen delays and some free time for relaxation.

Consistency: Establish a routine that suits you and follow it regularly with minor adjustments. This can help you develop habits and save time.

Clarity: Define your goal in each time block to maintain focus and motivation.

By mastering the art of time organization and utilizing the hour structuring technique, you can navigate the complexities of college life with greater ease and efficiency.

Making Your Schedule Visible and Accessible

Structuring your hours and managing your time effectively involves more than just creating a schedule—it's also crucial to keep that schedule visible and accessible. Here are some tips on how to do it:

- **Digital vs. Physical:** Decide whether you prefer digital scheduling apps or a physical planner. Both have their advantages, so choose the one that works best for you.
- **Color Coding:** Use color-coding techniques to distinguish between different types of tasks or commitments. For example, use one color for classes, another for work, and another for personal time.
- **Sync Devices:** If you use digital tools, make sure to sync your schedule across all your devices— computer, smartphone, and tablet. This ensures you can access your schedule anytime, anywhere.
- **Display It:** If you opt for a physical planner, keep it in a visible place in your dorm room or study area. A wall calendar with your schedule can serve as a daily reminder.
- **Set Reminders:** Use alarms and reminders on your devices to prompt you when it's time to transition between tasks or activities.
- **Share with Accountability Partners:** If you have study partners or accountability buddies, consider

sharing your schedule with them. This can help you stay on track and support each other's productivity.

- **Regular Updates:** Regardless of your scheduling method, remember to update it regularly to reflect any changes in your commitments or priorities.
- **Accessibility Tools:** Explore apps and tools designed for individuals with ADHD or organizational challenges. These tools often include features like visual schedules and reminders.

By making your schedule visible and accessible, you'll enhance your ability to stick to it and make the most of your structured hours. This practice can significantly contribute to your academic success and overall well-being.

Remember that effective time management is an ongoing process, and finding the right strategies and tools that work for you may take some experimentation. Stay flexible, adapt your schedule as needed, and keep striving for productivity and balance in your college life.

Avoiding procrastination

Procrastination is a term that likely strikes a chord with you. It's like a mysterious shadow that hovers around college campuses, ready to trap unsuspecting students. While it may seem like an inevitable part of student life, it's more akin to a puzzle waiting to be solved with the right approach. Let's discover how to outsmart this formidable obstacle and regain control of your academic journey.

Igniting Interest in Mundane Tasks

Now, what about those seemingly dull, uninspiring tasks? Lack of interest can often be the culprit behind procrastination. However, you can infuse purpose into even the most mundane endeavors with a dash of creativity. It might be about personal satisfaction, the opportunity to learn something new, or the excitement of achieving a top-notch grade. Remind yourself of the benefits, and you'll uncover that spark that rekindles your motivation.

Taming the Temptation of Distractions

Ah, distractions, the crafty seducers of productivity! Social media, friends, food, and sleep can beckon to you like sirens at sea. To resist their allure, create an environment that resembles a personal study haven. Power down those electronic devices, seek a cozy, distraction-free spot, or surround yourself with focused peers. Transform your study routine into an engaging treasure hunt, and you'll develop greater resistance to these common distractions.

Navigating the Waters of Disorganization

Disorganization and confusion can cast a spell of procrastination. If you ever find yourself adrift in a sea of information, it's time to become the captain of your study ship. Gather your materials, clarify instructions, and deploy tools that are trusty navigational aids. Calendars, planners, or specialized apps can become your steadfast allies in this quest for clarity and order.

Remember, procrastination isn't an impossible curse; it's a habit that can be reshaped and refined. These strategies are your magical keys to unlock a more productive and joyful college experience. Allow them to guide you, and you'll discover that procrastination becomes a myth of the past, enabling you to embrace the exhilarating learning adventure fully. With these newfound skills, you'll set sail toward academic success with the wind at your back and the open sea of knowledge before you.

Strategies for Balancing Academic and Social Life

Prioritize Tasks: Clearly distinguish between urgent/important tasks and social activities.

Set Clear Boundaries: Allocate specific times for studying and socializing. Stick to these schedules.

Use a Planner: Organize your tasks and social events in a planner to visualize and manage your time effectively.

Study Groups: Combine socializing with studying by forming or joining study groups.

Reward System: Reward yourself with social activities after completing study goals.

Digital Tools: Utilize apps that help track tasks and limit social media use during study hours.

Mindfulness Practices: Engage in mindfulness to stay focused and reduce the urge to procrastinate.

Regular Breaks: Take short breaks during study sessions to refresh and avoid burnout.

Set Realistic Goals: Avoid overcommitting; set achievable study and social goals.

Reflect on Consequences: Consider the long-term impact of procrastination on academic goals.

Balancing Priorities: Essential Skills for College and Beyond

In college, learning to balance academic responsibilities with a buzzing social life is about more than just immediate success; it's a crucial life skill. The ability to effectively prioritize during college lays a strong foundation for your future, especially in professional settings where distractions and demands on your time are constant. By mastering the art of prioritization and tactfully managing social commitments, you develop a skill set that ensures success beyond the university gates. It enables you to navigate life's varied challenges, maintain focus on your goals, and achieve a fulfilling and organized life. This includes learning to politely decline or exit social situations, a skill equally valuable in professional environments.

Politely declining or exiting social situations requires tact and honesty.

Here are some strategies:

Honesty with Tact: Be honest about your need to focus on your studies but express it tactfully. For example, "I'd love to join, but I have an important exam to prepare for."

Offer Alternatives: Suggest an alternative time for socializing. For instance, "I can't make it tonight, but how about we catch up this weekend?"

Use Positive Language: Frame your refusal positively, like, "I'm really committed to acing this project right now, but let's plan something soon!"

Short and Sweet: Keep your response brief and to the point, avoiding over-explanation.

Gratitude: Show appreciation for the invitation, "Thanks for thinking of me! I wish I could join."

Set Priorities: Occasionally remind your friends of your priorities so they understand your commitments.

Quick Exit Strategy: If you're already at an event, excuse yourself politely, perhaps saying you have an early day or study plans.

3 FROM FRESHMAN TO FINISH LINE

Books are your trusty sidekicks for anyone stepping into the vast universe of knowledge that is a college education. Like the beat of a hummingbird's wing, they flit about, filled with the nectar of wisdom, skills, bursts of inspiration, a good laugh when you need one, and often a shoulder to lean on in the form of motivation.

However, there's a different side to this coin. Books, especially those necessary to feed the academic beast, aren't always gentle on your pocket. This doesn't mean your learning journey should suffer. There are multiple paths to owning those all-important texts without emptying your bank account.

Acquiring Textbooks Without Breaking the Bank

Go Digital:

- Before you commit your dollars to that textbook, why not take a moment to explore the virtual marketplace? Websites and applications exist to help you compare book prices from various vendors. Think Amazon, Chegg, AbeBooks, and BookFinder. Let's not forget about price trackers, too. CamelCamelCamel or Honey are perfect assistants that watch price histories, alerting you when prices sink, or a sale is on. This digital exercise could be your key to great savings and free time.

Secondhand Doesn't Mean Second-Best:

- An effective strategy to save your pennies is to go for used books. Sure, they're not brand new, but often in good shape. Specialized websites such as ThriftBooks, Better World Books, and Alibris are brimming with secondhand books waiting for a new home. Or you could turn to fellow students who have walked the path you are on now. Social media, online forums, bulletin boards, or even a chat over coffee could land you some used books at affordable prices.

The Older Edition Advantage:

- The latest edition of a book isn't always the superior one. Older versions are often just as good and considerably lighter on the wallet. But check with your professor if using older editions will serve your purpose. Professors sometimes insist on the latest edition for their updated content. If you get a thumbs up for older editions, double-check the layout—page numbers, chapters, sections—to ensure they align with the newest edition.

Share and Care:

- Have you considered getting your hands on those books without spending a dime? It's doable. Your school library could be a treasure chest of textbooks you need. Borrow, use, return. Rinse and repeat. And then there's the idea of sharing with your classmates. Cost-sharing a book or an exchange system can work wonders. Plus, it opens up avenues for group study and learning from each other.

Exploring Low-Cost and Free Alternatives:

- If owning books feels too heavy on the pocket, you could explore low-cost or free alternatives.
- Digital Copies or Alternative Editions: Some generous authors or publishers might offer digital

versions or different editions of their books for free or at a fraction of the cost of the printed versions.

- Open Educational Resources (OER): This is a world of teaching and learning resources open to anyone with internet access. It's a universe where textbooks, courses, videos, podcasts, and simulations coexist for free use, modification, and sharing. Websites like OpenStax, OER Commons, and MERLOT are your gateways to this world.
- Library Databases: Your school library might have access to databases housing academic journals, articles, ebooks, and more. These can be the perfect supplement or even replacements for your textbooks.
- Course Reserves: Your professor might put some books on reserve in your school library. These high-demand or pricey books are for your use within the library for a limited period.

The price tag of books needn't weigh down the journey of a college student. There are many secret paths to owning the books you need for your courses without draining your finances. From exploring digital options and secondhand sources to embracing older editions and sharing with class-mates, these tips and strategies ensure you can have and read your books without duplicating efforts or information.

Study Methods

Unleashing your brain's full capacity for learning can become your secret superpower in academics. Yet, many grapple with finding the golden key to unlock their ability to absorb, process, and remember information for their course-work and exams. Since the landscape of learning styles is as diverse as our fingerprints, finding a universal key is unrealistic. However, we can forge some versatile tools to aid our quest for knowledge. Let's shine a light on some of these tools.

Experience the Pomodoro Study Technique

This time management approach offers a remarkable solution by promoting short, concentrated periods of effort interspersed with brief moments of relaxation. The rhythm of work and rest boosts your mental agility, drive, and effectiveness. Sounds exciting? All you need is a timer, a writing instrument, and paper. Here is the path to undertake:

First, pick a task or topic that's on your study list. Launch your timer for a set duration of 25 minutes and engage fully with your study material. Stay committed to your work, dodging distractions that might arise. When your timer buzzes, it's time to pause. Put a tick on your paper indicating a completed study burst, and step into a 5-minute rest interval. This is your opportunity to stretch, hydrate, or do something soothing.

Continue to replicate this rhythm until you have accumulated four Pomodoros—translating to 100 minutes of dedicated work with 15 minutes of relaxation. Post four Pomodoros, indulge in an extended break of 15 to 30 minutes. This time, gift yourself with an enjoyable activity. Carry forward this cycle with the next task on your list until you reach the end of your study session.

The beauty of the Pomodoro technique is that it actively discourages exhaustion, monotony, and weariness that often accompany extensive study sessions. Additionally, it offers a tangible means to track your progress and utilize your time effectively.

Let's Understand the Feynman Technique

Turning our attention to another effective study tool, we have the Feynman technique. This method strengthens your grasp of intricate concepts and amplifies your communication skills. Named after Richard Feynman, a recipient of the Nobel Prize in Physics, this technique is renowned for its simplicity in explaining abstract ideas. The Feynman technique's underlying principle is that teaching something to someone else fosters superior learning. By taking on the mantle of a teacher, you can spot any holes or misconceptions in your understanding and develop ways to simplify and demystify them. Here's how you can implement the Feynman Technique:

Select a concept that you wish to comprehend better. Visualize that you are explaining it to someone unfamiliar with the subject matter. This person could be a friend, a relative, or a fictitious entity. The key is to describe the concept in straightforward language, deploying practical examples or diagrams when required. Remember to abstain from using technical terms or complicated formulas. Once your explanation is ready, scrutinize it to identify any segments you find difficult to explain lucidly. Refer to your source material for additional information or examples to fill these gaps. Keep iterating through this process until you can confidently and precisely articulate the concept.

The Feynman technique is a powerful tool that deepens your understanding of any subject and boosts your critical thinking and problem-solving capabilities. It's particularly beneficial when preparing for exams, presentations, or interviews, as it enhances your ability to express yourself clearly and succinctly.

The Power of Mind Mapping

The final study tool in this section (not the least by any means) that you can add to your repertoire is mind mapping. It is a strategy that utilizes words and images to craft strong associations to aid your recall of the study material. Many find mind mapping a more intuitive form of note-taking, as it can be employed for brainstorming, planning, summarizing, and more.

The premise of mind mapping rests on the theory that our brains better absorb information when presented in a visual and creative format instead of a linear, logical structure. By employing colors, symbols, pictures, and keywords, you can capture and organize your ideas in a manner that resonates with you and stimulates your creativity.

To create a mind map:

Begin with a central topic or idea that encapsulates your aim to learn or study.

Add branches from the center, each representing subtopics or keywords linked to the main topic.

Expand these branches further to include more details or examples as required. You can also incorporate images, icons, or doodles to illustrate your points or trigger your memory.

Mind mapping can bolster your memory, creativity, and comprehension while studying. It also helps you perceive the overall image and the links between distinct concepts or topics. You can craft mind maps manually using paper and pens or opt for online platforms that offer more features and flexibility. Online tools enable you to modify, share, and collaborate on your mind maps and export them in PDF, Word, or PowerPoint formats. Visit Biggerplate at http://www.biggerplate.com/ for a wealth of resources, templates, and tutorials to supercharge your learning and organization.

Remember that different techniques may resonate more with certain subjects or scenarios. So, don't stop experimenting with them and discovering what aligns best with your learning style.

Practical Application vs. Active Reading

As you embark on your academic journey, you'll be surrounded by a vast sea of text. These written works, whether textbooks, essays, reports, or captivating novels, hold the keys to your kingdom of knowledge. Every word, sentence, and paragraph within these texts offer valuable insights, honing your ability to think critically, analyze deeply, and communicate effectively. But here's the twist – not every text reveals its secrets similarly. That's where our discussion on reading strategies comes in, particularly practical application and active reading.

The practical application serves as a bridge, connecting the theoretical wisdom you gain from texts to the practical realities of life. It's about transforming textual knowledge into a practical tool you can confidently wield in the real world. With practical application, the text springs to life, enhancing your motivation, piquing your interest, and elevating the overall joy of reading.

Consider these scenarios:

Utilizing a mathematical concept or formula from a textbook to solve a real-world problem.

Crafting a persuasive email to a government official using the logic and evidence you've gleaned from an article.

Creating a product or service based on the instructions or principles found in a manual.

Performing a scene from a play to bring the characters and themes envisioned by the author to life.

Now, let's venture into the realm of active reading. This strategy invites you to engage intimately with the text. It's a deliberate dance where you interact with each line, enhancing your comprehension, retention, and analytical skills. Active reading sharpens your focus, boosts your memory, and empowers you to form well-grounded opinions.

Here are some active reading techniques to consider:

- Developing a repertoire of questions to ask before, during, and after reading, delving into the text's purpose, core ideas, and finer details.
- Taking notes with thoughts, summaries, or assessments in the margins crystallizes your understanding.
- Creating visual aids like outlines or flowcharts to better visualize and organize the presented information.
- Formulate your examination questions based on the text to put your understanding to the test.
- Sharing the knowledge you've gathered from the text with someone else to solidify your understanding and uncover any gaps.

Neither practical application nor active reading is a one-size-fits-all solution. As you navigate your academic journey, you'll discover that each text or situation may require a different approach. Therefore, remaining flexible, adaptable, and open to various reading techniques is crucial. By doing so, you'll find yourself reading, absorbing, and growing with every word you encounter.

Conquering Exams and Tests: Techniques for Effective Exam Preparation and Performance

Exams and tests are a significant part of the college experience, and your success in these assessments can greatly impact your overall academic performance. To conquer exams and tests effectively, you need a strategic approach that combines preparation, time management, and stress management. This section will delve into techniques to help you excel in your exams and perform at your best when it matters most.

Understand the Exam Format

One of the first steps in preparing for an exam is to thoroughly understand the format. Are you facing multiple-choice questions, essays, short answers, or a combination of these? Knowing what to expect can help you tailor your study plan accordingly. Review any guidelines or rubrics provided by your professor.

Create a Study Schedule

Effective exam preparation begins with a well-structured study schedule. Start early to avoid last-minute cramming, which can lead to stress and decreased retention. Allocate specific time slots for each subject or topic, and be consistent in your study routine. This helps distribute your workload and prevents burnout.

Organize Your Study Material

Organize your study materials, notes, and resources to streamline your review process. Create clear and concise study guides or outlines for each subject or topic. Highlight key concepts, formulas, and definitions. Use color-coding or visual aids to make information more memorable.

Practice Active Learning

Passive reading and highlighting are not as effective as active learning techniques. Engage with the material by summarizing, questioning, and teaching it to yourself or others. Solve practice problems, write sample essays, and participate in study groups to reinforce your understanding.

Use Memory Techniques

Employ memory techniques such as mnemonic devices, acronyms, and visualization to enhance memory retention. Break down complex information into smaller, manageable chunks. Spaced repetition, where you review material at increasing intervals, is also an effective memory-enhancing strategy.

Take Practice Exams

Practice exams or mock tests are invaluable for assessing your knowledge and improving test-taking skills. Use past exam papers or online resources to simulate exam conditions. Time yourself to gauge your pace and identify areas where you need improvement.

Stay Healthy and Manage Stress

A healthy lifestyle plays a significant role in exam preparation. Get adequate sleep, maintain a balanced diet, and exercise regularly. Managing stress through relaxation techniques like deep breathing, meditation, or yoga can help you stay focused and calm during exams.

Foods to Boost Focus During Studying and Test-Taking

In addition to the techniques mentioned above, your diet can play a crucial role in enhancing concentration and mental clarity during studying and test-taking. Incorporate these brain-boosting foods into your routine:

Blueberries: Packed with antioxidants, blueberries improve memory and cognitive function. They are a perfect snack for study breaks.

Fatty Fish: Salmon, mackerel, and trout are rich in omega-3 fatty acids, which support brain health. They enhance memory and help maintain focus.

Dark Chocolate: Dark chocolate contains antioxidants and

caffeine, which can improve alertness and mood. Enjoy a small piece as a treat during study sessions.

Nuts and Seeds: Almonds, walnuts, and flaxseeds provide essential nutrients like vitamin E and omega-3s. They promote clear thinking and memory retention.

Leafy Greens: Spinach, kale, and other leafy greens are high in vitamins and minerals. They boost cognitive function and protect the brain from age-related decline.

Whole Grains: Opt for whole grains like oats and quinoa, which release glucose slowly into the bloodstream. This provides a steady supply of energy to the brain.

Berries: Strawberries, raspberries, and blackberries are rich in antioxidants and vitamin C. They help reduce stress and improve cognitive performance.

Avocado: Avocado is a source of healthy fats that support brain function. It also contains potassium, which enhances memory and concentration.

Turmeric: Curcumin, found in turmeric, has anti-inflamma-tory and antioxidant properties. It may improve memory and reduce brain fog.

Green Tea: Green tea contains L-theanine, an amino acid that promotes relaxation and focus without causing drowsiness.

Remember to stay hydrated by drinking plenty of water throughout your study sessions and exam days. Avoid excessive caffeine intake, which can lead to jitteriness and disrupt sleep. Instead, use herbal teas like chamomile or peppermint to stay calm and alert.

Incorporating these brain-boosting foods into your diet can enhance your cognitive abilities, improve focus, and support your overall academic success. Combine these dietary choices with effective study techniques and stress management strategies for optimal exam performance.

You Can Do So Much With Tutoring

Have you ever stumbled upon a hidden gem in the most unexpected places? Well, that's what tutoring is all about – uncovering hidden potentials. It's like a journey of self-discovery, where you unlock the treasures of knowledge hidden within you. But who are the wizards behind this magical process? They come in all forms – professors, fellow students, experts, and even volunteers – each with their unique way of making complex subjects seem as easy as pie.

Tutoring can happen anywhere – online, in the comfort of your dorm room, on the bustling campus, or even within small study groups where the energy is contagious.

Now, let's clear up a common misconception. Tutoring isn't the same as teaching. Teaching covers many topics, while tutoring serves bite-sized portions, focusing only on your needs. Are those math problems starting to resemble secret codes? Do you want to boost your grades or just need some extra practice? Think of tutoring as a tailor-made learning experience designed just for you.

The fascinating thing about tutoring is its flexibility. There are different styles to suit your preferences. In one-on-one tutoring, you take the center stage. Here, the pace of learning is entirely up to you, ensuring that the lessons are perfectly tailored to your unique needs. It's like having a custom-made suit of knowledge that fits you perfectly. And whether you prefer face-to-face interactions or virtual sessions, the choice is yours.

Then there's group tutoring. Imagine a small group of students, all with the same academic goals, learning together. This approach is fantastic if you enjoy studying with peers, love teamwork, or are mindful of your budget. Depending on what suits you best, you can choose between digital or in-person group sessions.

Peer tutoring is another interesting twist. Picture a fellow student, someone who's been in your shoes, sharing their wisdom. This helps ease the stress of exams and encourages active participation. These sessions often take place on campus or in the vast online realm.

Finding the right tutoring group might seem like a daunting task. But fear not! The digital world offers a plethora of possibilities. And don't forget to tap into your social network – your school, friends, and family might have excellent recommendations. When weighing your options, consider a few key factors – cost, quality, convenience, flexibility, and feedback.

Tutoring isn't just a service; it's a powerful tool. It bolsters your academic arsenal, taking you straight toward your learning goals. Once you discover the right tutoring group, you'll have an invaluable companion on your quest for knowledge. Plus, it adds a sprinkle of much-needed fun to the learning process. Who said learning can't be both work and play?

Knock Their Socks Off With a Well-Written College Paper!

Writing Winning College Papers

Ah, college papers—the classic academic challenge that beckons every student on their educational journey. Whether it's a research paper, an essay, or a critical analysis, mastering the art of writing these assignments can be a game-changer in your college experience. While it may seem daunting at first, rest assured that with the right strategies, anyone can become proficient at crafting well-researched, eloquent papers that not only earn top grades but also show-case your intellect and analytical skills. This chapter will explore the key steps to help you confidently conquer your college papers.

Crafting a Clear and Concise Thesis Statement

Every outstanding college paper commences with a crisp, direct thesis statement—an illuminating guide that steers your reader through your argument. Your thesis should encapsulate the core concept of your paper within a single sentence, serving as the linchpin that maintains your writing's focus and coherence.

To fashion an effective thesis statement, adhere to these principles:

Be Precise: Steer clear of vague statements; precisely identify the subject of your paper.

Quantify Your Claim: Your thesis should present a stance that is open to examination and assessment.

Keep It Feasible: Ensure your thesis is attainable within the parameters of your paper.

Relevance Is Paramount: The thesis should directly pertain to your topic.

Establish a Timeline: If pertinent, define a timeframe for your argument within the paper.

2. Back Up Your Thesis Statement

Once you've established your thesis, your paper's body serves as the support structure for your argument. Each paragraph should provide evidence, examples, and analysis to validate your thesis statement. This is where critical thinking skills come into play as you dissect your chosen topic, consider various perspectives, and provide well-researched evidence to strengthen your position.

3. Build an Outline

Before diving headfirst into writing, create a well-structured outline. Outlining helps you organize your thoughts, ensuring that your paper flows logically. Start with a strong introduction, then body paragraphs discussing a distinct point, and conclude with a compelling summary of your main arguments.

4. The First Draft

Don't agonize over achieving perfection in your initial draft. The primary purpose of this stage is to get your ideas down on paper. Write freely, and don't fret over minor errors or language intricacies. Once your thoughts are on the page, you can revise and refine them.

5. Write the Introduction Last

Although the introduction is the first part of your paper that your reader encounters, it's often best to write it last. By waiting until you've completed the body of your paper, you can craft an introduction that accurately reflects the content and direction of your essay.

In your introduction, aim to:

Engage the Reader: Use a captivating hook to pique your reader's interest.

Provide Context: Offer background information to contextualize your topic.

State Your Thesis: Present your thesis statement.

Outline Your Approach: Briefly describe how your paper will unfold.

6. Editing and Proofreading

After completing your first draft, step back and give yourself some time before revising. This break allows you to return to your work with fresh eyes, making it easier to spot errors, inconsistencies, and areas for improvement. During the editing process:

Check for Clarity: Ensure your ideas are clearly expressed, and your argument flows logically.

Refine Your Language: Eliminate unnecessary words, use precise vocabulary, and vary sentence structure to enhance readability.

Review Grammar and Style: Pay attention to punctuation, grammar, and formatting rules.

Seek Feedback: Consider sharing your paper with a peer or professor for constructive criticism.

While AI tools can be beneficial for obtaining suggestions and feedback during the editing process, it's essential to clarify that they should never be used to generate the paper from start to finish. AI can aid in enhancing your work, but it should complement your writing, not replace it.

7. Citation and References

College papers often require citing sources to support your arguments. Be sure to follow the citation style specified by your instructor, whether it's APA, MLA, Chicago, or another format. Keep meticulous records of your sources and their page numbers to facilitate proper citation.

8. Proofreading and Final Touches

Before submitting your paper, conduct a final proofread. Carefully examine grammar, spelling, and punctuation. You can also utilize tools like Grammarly or other websites that help you identify common grammar issues. Ensure your paper follows formatting guidelines, such as margins, font size, and line spacing. Additionally, double-check that your citations are accurate and complete. This meticulous review ensures that your paper is polished and ready for submission.

9. Seek feedback

Don't hesitate to contact professors, tutors, or writing centers for guidance and feedback. Constructive criticism can immensely benefit your writing and help you refine your skills.

10. Conclusion

Writing winning college papers is a skill that takes time to develop. Still, with practice and dedication, you can master it. Remember that each paper you write is an opportunity to showcase your critical thinking, research prowess, and communication ability. Embrace the writing process, and you'll earn top grades and gain valuable skills that will serve you well throughout your academic and professional journey.

Walking Tall in College

Imagine yourself in a college classroom, your heart fluttering like a bird poised for its inaugural flight, palms slightly damp. The room thrums with intellectual prowess, the aura of accomplishment almost palpable. Suddenly, uncertainty taps your shoulder. Is this environment truly for you? Are you capable of tackling these challenges and flourishing? Banish that fear, dear reader, for your potential is boundless; you just need a sprinkle of academic confidence.

The Essence of Academic Confidence

Forget buzzwords; academic confidence is your magic carpet, lifting you above mountains of academic challenges. It fuels motivation, engagement, performance, and personal well-ness in college. It protects against anxiety, stress, laziness, avoidance, and poor results. The million-dollar question arises: how do you acquire this potent potion of success?

1. Self and Peer Assessment

Embrace self-assessment as the camera that throws back your progress in high definition. Pair it with peer assessment. Together, they offer a clear lens that enhances your academic vision, providing insights into your strengths, weaknesses, and opportunities for growth.

2. Constructive Feedback

Feedback isn't meant to reduce your efforts to rubble but to build bridges from your current state to your could-be excellence. Seek timely, specific, balanced, actionable, and respectful feedback, and watch your academic confidence take flight.

3. Clearing the Mental Clutter

Allow your mind some breathing space. Bid farewell to self-doubt, anxiety, stress, guilt, and shame. Breathe in positivity via exercises like meditation, journaling, or seeking trusted confidants. Create a space for creativity and problem-solving, and let the radiance of confidence pierce through.

4. Positivity: Your Shield Against Negativity

Arm yourself with positivity, your shield against negativity from various sources. Replace doubts with affirmations, confront critics gracefully, and tackle stress like a seasoned warrior.

5. The Power of Vulnerability

Recognize that seeking help is not a sign of weakness but a display of strength. Let guidance, encouragement, and advice be your allies in the battleground of academia. Your growth and confidence will be better for it.

6. Micro-Confidence: The Building Blocks of Success

Cherish the small but significant acts that constitute micro-confidence. They are the building blocks of a towering edifice of self-assurance, resilience, and success.

7. Nurturing Pride

Plant seeds of achievements and water them with appreciation. Witness them bloom into a lush garden of motivation, satisfaction, and confidence.

8. Aligning With Passion

Align your academic path with your values, interests, and passions. Let them be your guide, leading you toward fulfillment and joy.

You are now armed with the tools to tackle the college experience with academic confidence as your guide. Employ these techniques and watch your transformation into a confident scholar, prepared to explore, learn, and conquer. Your college success story is yours to write; the pen is in your hand. Create your masterpiece.

Forming friendships, connecting with professors and tutors, and weaving yourself into the colorful fabric of college life—these do not have to be a struggle. If the initial chapters haven't quite drawn you into the joyful dance of campus living, perhaps this third attempt will strike the right chord and guide you into the rhythm of academic enjoyment.

4 FINDING YOUR VOICE

The only journey is the one within. –Rainer Maria
Rilke

Navigating the college campus can sometimes
make forming connections feel like venturing
into uncharted territory. As you look around, it
might seem like everyone else has effortlessly found their
place, leaving you feeling like a puzzle piece that doesn't
quite fit. Surprisingly, this sense of unease is quite common,
with approximately 53% of students sharing these feelings
(according to Gen Z College, 2022). But there's no need to
worry. This chapter serves as your reliable guide to creating
genuine connections and engaging in meaningful conversations. Within these pages, you'll uncover the art of forging

friendships that flow as naturally as breathing. Armed with the insights found here, you'll nurture connections that not only fill your social landscape but also enrich your life, transforming moments of solitude into a beautiful symphony of friendships and meaningful encounters.

Vanquishing Social Isolation

Emily stood at the threshold of a brand-new chapter in her life, her dorm room symbolizing endless possibilities. College felt like an exciting adventure with a mix of excitement, a touch of uncertainty, and just a hint of nerves. As she looked around at her unfamiliar surroundings, her heart raced with anticipation. College, with its vast landscape, beckoned to her, an introvert ready to tackle its challenges.

During her early college days, Emily became a devoted bookworm and a curious learner. Her room was like a library, filled with the well-loved scent of novels. While her peers were out making friends, her companions were the characters from her favorite books. Her happiness was a solitary one, shared only with the authors of those beloved stories. But as she watched her lively classmates effortlessly making connections, something inside her stirred—a deep desire to be a part of that tapestry of relationships.

Her adventurous spirit led her to a book club, where she felt a bit hesitant at first but soon found fellow book lovers who shared her passion. It was like watching a hidden flower slowly bloom, finding its place among kindred souls. Yet, some nights brought a sense of solitude to Emily. While others reveled in joy and laughter, she sometimes felt the pull of loneliness, aware that she was still within her self-imposed boundaries. But Emily was determined to break free. She reached out to others, starting with a simple coffee date with her roommate, which turned into an afternoon of revelations and shared dreams. That coffee date marked the beginning of a beautiful friendship.

Before long, an invitation to a party arrived, a beacon of light in the midst of her hesitation. Parties were uncharted territory for Emily, but wasn't college all about exploring the unknown? Encouraged by her newfound friend, she not only picked out an outfit but also gathered newfound courage. Stepping into the party felt like turning a page in her life's story. Amidst the noise and chaos, Emily discovered kindred spirits—fellow introverts, each a unique note in a symphony of shared moments. They talked, laughed, and intertwined their lives. Weeks turned into cherished memories, and Emily began to bloom. Her connections, though few, were deep and meaningful. Solitude was gradually replaced by a sense of belonging. She found her rhythm, her melody, and, most importantly, she found herself.

For Emily, college wasn't just a series of hallways or a class schedule; it was a vast canvas, and she was its artist. She was ready to infuse her world with color, one inspired brushstroke at a time.

Solitude: An Oasis and a Mirage

Discovering the beauty of spending time alone is like finding your favorite tune—a peaceful rhythm of self-reflection, relaxation, and getting to know yourself better. Dive into the enchanting world of a good book, the comfort of your favorite songs, or the joy of pursuing your hobbies solo. Your personal space can become a cozy and empowering retreat.

But, it's important to navigate this path carefully because too much alone time can sometimes lead to isolation. College is all about growth and new experiences, and those experiences often come from interactions with others. While enjoying your "me time" is great, you don't want it to become a wall that keeps you from connecting with people.

It's reassuring to know that many students, just like you, go through similar feelings. Understanding that loneliness is something many people experience can be the first step in finding a balance and reducing some of the stress that comes with it. Feeling a bit out of place in a new environment is perfectly normal.

So, don't hesitate to reach out and start a conversation. You might be surprised to find that your seemingly quiet neighbor or the person eating alone in the cafeteria is also looking for social connections. By sharing your thoughts and experiences, you can build strong bonds and turn your college journey into a harmonious ensemble, rather than a solo performance.

The Power of Groups and New Interests

College is a vibrant stage, brimming with opportunities to participate in group activities and explore new hobbies. These platforms serve as your golden tickets, leading you to potential comrades and the chance to forge meaningful friendships. Whether it's joining a sports team, participating in a drama group, or getting involved in a charity organization, engaging in these spaces can connect you with individuals who resonate with your interests.

Don't hesitate to experiment and step outside of your comfort zone. College serves as the ideal rehearsal ground for venturing into uncharted territories. You may find that the most unlikely pursuits can ignite your passion and lead you toward unexpected and enriching friendships.

Reach Out to Your Cheer Squad

Distance doesn't diminish the significance of your relationships back home. Your family and friends continue to be your enthusiastic supporters, even when miles separate you. Thanks to technology, the world feels smaller than ever, allowing you to maintain the vitality of your cherished bonds through regular calls, video chats, or heartfelt text messages.

These connections offer solace, guidance, and a stable anchor during moments of solitude, enabling you to navigate the challenges of college life.

Facing solitude in college can initially seem like a daunting solo performance. However, it has the potential to evolve into an enriching ensemble experience with the right approach. Embracing solitude without losing your sense of self, recognizing that others share similar feelings, exploring various groups and hobbies, sharing your interests with peers, and staying connected with your support system back home can transform the initial apprehension into a harmonious and fulfilling melody.

Check-Ins: Staying Connected

The college journey marks not just a change in scenery but a transformation in the dynamics of family life. As college students explore new horizons, face challenges, and experience personal growth, their parents also embark on a journey of their own, shifting from caregivers to supportive advisors. The physical distance that often separates families, spanning cities, states, or even countries, need not create an emotional divide. On the contrary, it offers an enriching opportunity to redefine and strengthen the parent-child connection.

But how can you navigate this change effectively? Allow me to guide you through this process.

Communication: It's not merely about routine conversations; it's about meaningful exchanges of emotions, achievements, struggles, and words of encouragement. Striking the right balance between quality and frequency is essential, whether through heartfelt phone calls, thoughtful emails, or lively video chats. It's about more than just talking; it's about truly connecting, understanding, and bridging the miles between you.

Visits: These are not just opportunities to see each other but moments of shared experiences, understanding, laughter, and love. Planning visits requires more than coordination; it demands flexibility, openness, and a genuine eagerness to immerse yourself in each other's worlds, whether on a bustling college campus or in the comfort of your hometown.

Celebrations: Special occasions are not mere dates on a calendar; they are milestones filled with love, pride, joy, and lasting memories. Thoughtfully commemorating these moments through heartfelt gifts, virtual gatherings, or in-person festivities contributes to a shared history and a continued sense of unity.

These strategies are not just methods but pathways to nurturing a deeper, more meaningful connection. While physical separation may initially appear challenging and stressful, it does not have to be a barrier. With open hearts, a willingness to adapt, and an eagerness to connect, parents and students can build a relationship that not only endures but flourishes. Embrace this transition with grace, wisdom, and hope, for the distance that may feel like a gap today can be the very thing that brings you closer tomorrow.

Navigating College Relationships

Amidst the vibrant whirlwind of college life, the friendships you cultivate become not only your steadfast anchor but also the pillars of your support system. These bonds infuse your college journey with companionship, laughter, and inspiration, motivating you to excel academically while enhancing your overall social and emotional well-being.

However, it's essential to recognize that not every college friendship is akin to a four-leaf clover. Some relationships may prove unhealthy, toxic, superficial, or misaligned with your personal goals and values. Therefore, as you navigate this exciting phase of life, it's paramount to prioritize friendships that enrich your existence and drive you toward success.

Initiating a conversation serves as your initial stride toward establishing these meaningful connections. The art of conversation serves as the foundation of any strong friendship. It grants you the opportunity to express yourself, share your interests, opinions, and life experiences, while also gaining insight into the person across from you. These exchanges lay the groundwork for trust and respect, both vital elements in fostering a healthy friendship. Thus, present yourself as friendly, approachable, and respectful. Exhibit curiosity, attentiveness, and responsiveness. Utilize open-ended questions, compliments, humor, and shared interests to initiate and sustain engaging conversations.

Now, let's delve into expanding your social circles. An excellent approach to achieve this is by participating in clubs or organizations that resonate with your interests or aspirations. These platforms introduce you to individuals who share your passions, providing opportunities to partake in meaningful activities, acquire new skills, and contribute to your community. To identify the right club or organization for you, conduct thorough research about the offerings on your campus, attend events that align with your interests, and engage actively.

Furthermore, it's vital to remember that the friendships you have already established hold immense value. Nurturing these existing bonds is just as significant as forging new ones. Built upon mutual understanding and care, these connections bring depth and richness to your social landscape, rendering them stronger and more gratifying. Staying in touch, displaying genuine interest in your friends' lives, expressing gratitude, and celebrating their achievements are all ways to deepen these connections and make them more meaningful.

The Joys of Diversity

College is a tapestry woven with the vibrant threads of cultures, identities, and perspectives, each contributing to a colorful mosaic of diversity. This richness is not merely decorative; it serves as a dynamic force, enhancing your education and shaping you into a well-rounded individual prepared to navigate a multicultural world. However, the presence of diversity alone does not guarantee a fruitful environment. In this context, cultivating diverse friendships and nurturing an atmosphere of respect and inclusivity among your peers can yield numerous benefits for your personal and social development.

One remarkable advantage of diverse friendships is their ability to ignite creativity. As you immerse yourself in the myriad colors of these relationships, your mind becomes a fertile ground for fresh ideas, intriguing insights, and enriching experiences. It's a mental gym where your imagination receives a vigorous workout, fostering curiosity and innovation. Embracing diversity encourages you to engage with different viewpoints and critically evaluate evidence, transforming you into an intellectually flexible individual equipped with the skills demanded by modern careers and academic success.

Maintaining a diverse circle of friends also functions as a cross-cultural workshop, honing your ability to interact with individuals from various cultural backgrounds. This engagement allows you to delve into the fascinating realms of diverse cultures, languages, values, and beliefs, all while offering glimpses of your own cultural tapestry. These interactions dispel stereotypes, prejudices, and biases, replacing them with empathy, respect, and a profound appreciation for cultural diversity. The outcome is your emergence as a global citizen, characterized by tolerance, open-mindedness, and inclusivity.

Another invaluable aspect of these friendships is personal growth. As you reflect on both your commonalities and distinctions with your friends, you gain a deeper understanding of yourself, your strengths, and your values. Willingness to venture into uncharted territory leads to an expansion of your comfort zone, a reassessment of your assumptions, and the acquisition of skills to navigate ambiguity.

To truly experience the magic of diversity, you must foster an environment of respect and inclusivity. It involves creating a space where everyone feels at home, regardless of their background, culture, identity, or perspective. Picture it as orchestrating the diverse musical notes into a harmonious symphony, where each unique sound is cherished and celebrated. Here are some practical steps to achieve this:

- Explore your own cultural identity and biases while appreciating the diversity around you.
- Display genuine curiosity and a willingness to learn from those who differ from you.
- Exhibit consideration in all your interactions.
- Promote collaboration and mutual support in your activities.
- Be open to adjusting your attitudes and opinions.
- Let empathy and compassion guide your feelings and actions towards others.

By embracing these principles, you can create a thriving environment that not only celebrates diversity but also cultivates a profound sense of unity and understanding among all its members.

Standing Up for Yourself

Let's talk about assertive communication—a skill that can truly be a game-changer for your college journey. It's all about finding that sweet spot between respect and straight-forwardness, allowing you to express your needs and feelings in a clear and considerate manner. This skill will not only enhance your relationships but also sharpen your communication abilities, ultimately propelling you closer to your academic and personal goals.

Picture this: you're engaged in a lively discussion with your peers, tackling various topics and sharing your viewpoints. Now, speaking up confidently in such situations can be a bit daunting, especially when your thoughts differ from the popular consensus or face resistance. But fear not, because here are some strategies to help you ace it:

- Embrace the "I" perspective. Instead of saying, "You're incorrect," try something like, "I see it differently." This small shift keeps the conversation centered around your ideas, avoiding the potential pitfalls of blame games or heated arguments.
- Build your arguments on facts. Swap out "This is terrible" with "This idea seems to have a few pitfalls..." By grounding your thoughts in solid reasoning, you maintain objectivity and avoid biased judgments.
- Cultivate respect. Even in the midst of a passionate

discussion, it's important to prevent it from turning into a battle. Instead of dismissing an opposing view as "ridiculous," consider responding with, "That's a novel viewpoint; could you elaborate?" This approach fosters respect and keeps the door open for constructive dialogue.

With these assertive communication techniques in your toolbox, you'll be better equipped to navigate discussions, express your ideas confidently, and engage with your peers in a way that promotes mutual respect and understanding. So, go ahead and give it a try—it's a valuable skill that will serve you well throughout your college journey and beyond!

Roommate 101

Navigating Nudity with Roommates

Living with roommates often involves encountering their habits and preferences, including their comfort levels with nudity. While some individuals may feel at ease with nudity, others may find it uncomfortable or inappropriate. Addressing this situation effectively is essential for maintaining a respectful and tension-free living environment.

Practical Solutions:

Initiating an Honest Conversation

Initiating an Honest Conversation: Start by having an open and straightforward talk about the issue. Choose a time when you and your roommates can sit down and chat. Use relatable language and express your feelings honestly. For instance, say, "Hey, I've got to be real with you – seeing someone in the buff in our shared living room makes me pretty uncomfortable."

Encourage Open Dialogue

Encourage Your Roommates to Share: After you've shared your feelings, encourage your roommates to do the same. Make them feel comfortable discussing their comfort levels and boundaries regarding nudity. Show that you're willing to listen and understand where they're coming from.

Establish Clear Rules Together

Create Clear Rules Together: If needed, work together to create some simple and agreed-upon rules regarding nudity in common areas. These rules should respect everyone's comfort zones. You might say something like, "Can we all agree not to go au naturel in the living room? It'd make things a lot less awkward for everyone."

Define Private Spaces

Define Private Spaces: If you share a space, make sure to define which areas are considered "private" and "shared." Clearly mark where nudity is off-limits, so everyone knows where personal privacy is respected.

Show Mutual Respect

Respect Each Other: Once you've set up some ground rules, be sure to follow them. Show that you respect your roommates' boundaries and expect the same in return. A little respect can go a long way in making sure everyone feels comfortable at home.

By following these practical steps and having an open conversation in a relatable manner, you can address the issue of nudity with your roommates more effectively and promote mutual understanding and a peaceful living situation.

LGBTQ Roommates

Living with LGBTQ roommates can be a rewarding experience that offers the opportunity to learn, grow, and build meaningful relationships. To ensure a harmonious living situation and promote inclusivity, consider the following strategies:

Practical Solutions:

Educate Yourself about LGBTQ Experiences

Creating a safe and inclusive living environment starts with educating yourself about LGBTQ experiences, challenges, and identities. Make an effort to understand the terminology and correct usage of pronouns to ensure that you're respectful and sensitive in your interactions with LGBTQ roommates.

Initiate Open and Non-Judgmental Conversations

Initiate open and non-judgmental conversations about LGBTQ topics. Encourage your roommates to share their experiences, concerns, and perspectives. Be a good listener and express genuine interest in learning from them. By fostering a culture of respect and acceptance, you can create an environment where everyone feels valued and understood.

Avoid Making Assumptions

Avoid making assumptions about your LGBTQ roommates' experiences or identities. Instead, ask questions and seek clarification when needed. Understanding that everyone's journey is unique and that you may not fully grasp their experiences can help prevent conflicts and promote mutual respect.

Approach Conflicts with Patience and Empathy

In cases where conflicts or misunderstandings do arise, approach the situation with patience and empathy. Open dialogue is key to resolving conflicts related to LGBTQ issues. Remember that your LGBTQ roommates are individuals with their own stories and emotions, and it's important to treat them with the same respect and consideration you would expect in return.

By actively engaging with your LGBTQ roommates, educating yourself, and maintaining open communication, you can foster a supportive and harmonious living environment that values diversity and inclusivity.

Religious/Spiritual Issues

Religious and spiritual beliefs are deeply personal and can vary widely among individuals. When roommates with different belief systems come together, conflicts may arise over various aspects such as dietary requirements, decorations, daily rituals, and more. It's essential to navigate these differences with respect and understanding.

Practical Solutions:

Respect for Beliefs

Respect is the cornerstone of resolving conflicts related to religious or spiritual differences. Begin by acknowledging and respecting your roommates' beliefs, just as you expect them to respect yours. Understand that diversity in religious and spiritual practices is a part of a multicultural and inclusive living environment.

Open and Honest Communication

Initiate open and honest conversations about religious and spiritual practices. Share your own beliefs and practices while actively listening to your roommates' perspectives. This dialogue can help you gain insight into each other's values and needs.

Willingness to Compromise

In situations where conflicts arise, be willing to compromise. Find common ground that allows everyone to coexist peacefully. For example, if you have different dietary requirements due to religious beliefs, discuss how to store and prepare food in a way that accommodates both sets of dietary restrictions.

Creating Shared Spaces

Designate shared spaces where religious or spiritual practices can be performed without infringing on anyone else's comfort. This could include setting up a designated meditation area or prayer space within your living quarters.

Celebrating Diversity

Embrace the opportunity to learn about different religious and spiritual traditions. Participate in celebrations or ceremonies, if invited, to show your support and understanding.

Conflict Resolution

If conflicts related to religious or spiritual issues do arise, approach them with empathy and a willingness to find solutions that respect everyone's beliefs. Seeking the assistance of a mediator or residence advisor may be helpful in resolving complex conflicts.

By prioritizing respect, open communication, compromise, and inclusivity, you can navigate religious and spiritual differences with your roommates while maintaining a harmonious living environment that values diversity.

Sex, Masturbation, and Roommate Liaisons

Living in shared spaces may occasionally involve conflicts related to sexual activity, masturbation, or roommate liaisons. These situations can be sensitive and may lead to discomfort or tension if not addressed properly.

Practical Solutions:

Privacy Needs and Boundaries

Open and honest communication about privacy needs and boundaries is essential. Initiate a conversation with your roommates to discuss your expectations and preferences regarding privacy, especially in shared living areas. Encourage your roommates to do the same.

Establish Clear Ground Rules

If you have specific rules or expectations regarding sexual activity or masturbation, discuss and agree upon them with your roommates. Having clear, mutually agreed-upon ground rules can help prevent misunderstandings and conflicts.

Shared Spaces vs. Private Spaces

Distinguish between shared and private spaces within your living quarters. Clarify which areas are designated for personal privacy and which areas should be kept free from sexual activity.

Respect for Shared Spaces

Maintain respect for shared spaces by ensuring they remain clean and suitable for all roommates. If a sexual encounter occurs, ensure that it's conducted discreetly and in accordance with any established ground rules.

Open and Non-judgmental Communication

Encourage an environment where roommates can openly discuss their needs and concerns related to sexual activity. Avoid making assumptions about your roommates' preferences and comfort levels.

Conflict Resolution

In the event of a conflict or discomfort related to sexual activity, address the issue calmly and respectfully. Seek mutually agreeable solutions that prioritize everyone's comfort and privacy.

By fostering open communication, setting clear boundaries, and respecting each other's privacy needs, you can navigate issues related to sexual activity, masturbation, and roommate liaisons more effectively and maintain a harmonious living environment.

Building Trust and Addressing Lying/Stealing Issues with Roommates

Trust is the bedrock of any successful roommate relationship. However, when trust is violated through dishonesty, such as lying or stealing, it can lead to significant conflicts and a toxic living environment. To address these issues effectively, consider implementing practical solutions that promote trust, resolution, and harmonious cohabitation.

Practical Solutions:

Honest Conversations

Initiating an Honest Conversation: Begin by having open and honest conversations with your roommates. Choose a time when everyone can sit down and talk. Use straightforward and relatable language to express your feelings honestly. For example, you could say, "Hey, I need to be upfront with you – I've noticed some of my things have gone missing, and it's making me uneasy."

Encourage Accountability

Encourage your roommates to take responsibility for their actions. If one of them admits to lying or stealing, it's vital to discuss the consequences and express how it has affected you and the overall living situation. Fostering accountability can be a critical step in rebuilding trust.

Seek Mediation

When open communication alone doesn't resolve the issue, seeking mediation can be a sensible approach. A neutral third party, such as a mediator or counselor, can facilitate a constructive dialogue between roommates. Mediation provides a structured and safe environment for discussing concerns and working towards solutions.

Establish Boundaries and Agreements

To prevent future conflicts related to trust, consider creating clear boundaries and agreements with your roommates.

These agreements should include guidelines on respecting each other's privacy, property, and personal space. Put these boundaries in writing and ensure that all roommates agree and sign the document. This can serve as a reference point in case of future disagreements.

Promote Accountability and Transparency

Encourage a culture of accountability and transparency within your living space. Roommates should feel comfortable discussing their actions, concerns, and expectations openly. Regular check-ins or house meetings can be an effective way to maintain clear communication and ensure that everyone is on the same page.

Seek Professional Assistance

In cases where trust issues persist and negatively impact your living situation, consider seeking professional assistance. A counselor or therapist can help roommates address underlying issues contributing to the breach of trust and develop strategies for rebuilding a healthy living environment.

By implementing these practical solutions and focusing on open communication, accountability, and conflict resolution, you can work towards rebuilding trust with your roommates and maintaining a harmonious living environment. Trust is a vital component of roommate relationships, and addressing trust issues directly can lead to a healthier and more positive shared living experience.

Drunk or High Roommates

Living with roommates can bring together individuals with diverse views on substance use. While some may have no issue with it, others may find frequent intoxication disruptive or concerning. To maintain a harmonious household, it's crucial to address these differences in a respectful and proactive manner.

Practical Solutions:

Open and Honest Dialogue

Initiating an Honest Conversation: Begin by having an open and honest conversation with your roommates about substance use. Choose a time when everyone can engage in a calm and non-judgmental discussion. Use "I" statements to express your concerns and feelings. For instance, you might say, "I've noticed that frequent intoxication in our shared spaces affects my ability to focus on my responsibilities and makes me uncomfortable."

Establish Clear Boundaries

Work together to establish clear and mutually agreed-upon boundaries regarding substance use within shared spaces. Determine which areas are designated as "private" and where substance use is permitted or prohibited. Having written guidelines can help ensure that everyone's comfort zones are respected. You might agree, for example, that substance use is limited to individual bedrooms or specific common areas.

Promote Responsible Use

Encourage roommates who choose to engage in substance use to do so responsibly and respectfully. Emphasize the importance of moderation, safety, and consideration for others in shared living spaces. Encourage open dialogue about responsible substance use, and discuss the potential impacts on individual and collective responsibilities within the household.

Create a Schedule or Agreement

Consider creating a schedule or agreement for substance use within shared spaces. This can help ensure that intoxication doesn't interfere with roommate responsibilities, such as chores, study time, or shared activities. A schedule might include designated "quiet hours" during which substance use is discouraged to maintain a peaceful environment.

Express Concerns Calmly

If you have concerns about your roommates' substance use, address them calmly and respectfully. Avoid judgment or accusations. Instead, express your feelings and observations using "I" statements. For example, you could say, "I've noticed that when there's frequent intoxication in our shared spaces, it can lead to disruptions, and I'm concerned about our household's overall well-being."

Seek Mediation if Necessary

In cases where conflicts or misunderstandings persist, consider seeking mediation. A neutral third party, such as a counselor or mediator, can facilitate a constructive dialogue between roommates. Mediation provides a structured and unbiased platform for discussing concerns, finding compromises, and reaching agreements that support a peaceful living environment.

By implementing these practical solutions and emphasizing open communication, responsible behavior, and conflict resolution, you can navigate differences in substance use with your roommates more effectively. Creating a household where everyone's comfort, responsibilities, and concerns are respected is essential for maintaining a peaceful and harmonious living environment.

Messy Roommates

Differing standards of cleanliness among roommates can potentially result in conflicts and resentment. Addressing this issue effectively is vital for ensuring a harmonious living environment.

Practical Solutions:

Create a Cleaning Schedule

One practical approach to mitigate conflicts related to cleanliness is to create a cleaning schedule. Sit down with your roommates and allocate specific cleaning duties to each person. Establish a regular cleaning routine that includes tasks such as vacuuming, dusting, and bathroom cleaning. Make sure everyone is aware of their responsibilities and the schedule for completing them.

Divide Chores Equitably

When dividing cleaning chores, aim for equity. Consider each person's schedule, availability, and preferences when assigning tasks. Rotate responsibilities regularly to ensure that no one feels burdened or unfairly treated. For example, you can agree to switch chores every week or month to distribute the workload evenly.

Establish Clear Expectations

Communicate openly with your roommates about your expectations regarding cleanliness. Share your standards and preferences for a clean living space, and encourage your roommates to do the same. By understanding each other's perspectives, you can work towards a compromise that respects everyone's comfort levels.

Address Issues Promptly

If cleanliness issues arise, address them promptly but diplomatically. Avoid confrontations or accusations and instead opt for a calm and respectful conversation. Use "I" statements to express your concerns and feelings. For instance, you might say, "I've noticed that the kitchen hasn't been as clean as we agreed, and it's important to me that we all contribute to keeping our shared spaces tidy."

Accountability Check-Ins

Implement regular accountability check-ins with your roommates to assess the cleanliness of your shared spaces. During these check-ins, discuss whether everyone is fulfilling their cleaning duties and whether adjustments to the cleaning schedule or responsibilities are necessary. This practice helps maintain transparency and ensures that cleanliness remains a shared priority.

Celebrate Achievements

Recognize and celebrate achievements in maintaining a clean living space. Express appreciation for your roommates' contributions to cleanliness, and acknowledge when improvements have been made. Positive reinforcement can motivate everyone to continue working together to keep your shared areas tidy.

By applying these practical solutions and fostering open communication, equitable chore distribution, and a shared commitment to cleanliness, you can effectively address conflicts arising from differing cleanliness standards among roommates. Creating a clean and harmonious living environment that respects everyone's preferences and responsibilities is key to a peaceful cohabitation.

Chatty/Noisy Roommates

Diverse social needs among roommates can lead to conflicts, especially when one roommate prefers peace and quiet while the other tends to be chatty or noisy. Addressing this situation requires effective communication and compromise.

Practical Solutions:

Define Quiet Hours

To create a harmonious living environment, consider defining specific quiet hours during which noise should be minimized. Collaboratively decide on a reasonable time-frame for these quiet hours that accommodates everyone's needs. For instance, you can agree on quiet hours from 10:00 PM to 7:00 AM to ensure that everyone has an opportunity for uninterrupted rest.

Designate Quiet Zones

Designate specific areas within your living space as "quiet zones." For example, you can declare the living room or study area as a quiet zone where noise should be kept to a minimum. This allows roommates who require quiet to have dedicated spaces for solitude while still permitting social interaction in other areas.

Communicate Your Needs

Encourage open and honest communication about your social needs and preferences with your roommates. Express your desire for quiet or your need for social interaction calmly and respectfully. For instance, you can say, "I appreciate our conversations, but there are times when I need quiet to study or unwind."

Active Listening and Empathy

Practice active listening when your roommates express their social needs. Understand that everyone has different preferences, and it's essential to empathize with their perspectives. Engage in a constructive dialogue to find common ground that respects each other's requirements for social interaction and solitude.

Collaborate on Schedules

Collaboratively create schedules that accommodate both quiet and social hours. Negotiate specific times when you can expect some noise and other times when you can enjoy peace and quiet. This compromise ensures that everyone's needs are considered.

Utilize Noise-Canceling Options

For moments when noise is unavoidable, consider using noise-canceling headphones or white noise machines. These tools can help mitigate disturbances and provide you with the quiet atmosphere you need, even when your roommates are engaged in social activities.

By applying these practical solutions, which include establishing quiet hours, designating quiet zones, openly discussing social needs, and finding a balance through collaboration and compromise, you can effectively address conflicts related to chatty or noisy roommates. Creating an environment that respects varying social preferences while maintaining open communication is key to harmonious cohabitation.

Math, Mind, and Mentor: Olivia's Triumph

Unlike your typical math student, let's meet Olivia – a vibrant whirlwind of color and unpredictability. She had this incredible knack for finding beauty in numbers, patterns, and equations, sensing an enchanting harmony that connected everything from teeny-tiny particles to those faraway twinkling stars. But in this intricate mathematical waltz, she stumbled more than a few times. Math was like a captivating language she adored but didn't always grasp completely. Her curious mind wandered off, making it a tad challenging to keep up with her studies. The once-enticing world of math was slowly losing its charm, replaced by the icy clutches of self-doubt and fear.

Now, picture Professor Graham, the kind of teacher who could turn even the most baffling concepts into something as understandable as your favorite song lyrics. His students loved him not just for his genius but also for his down-to-earth warmth and humility.

Fast forward to Olivia's sophomore year, and she's suddenly hit with the cold, hard reality of failing grades and thoughts of giving up on her dream. The subject she once adored felt like an insurmountable mountain. But then, there was Professor Graham, noticing her stumbles and inviting her to his office one day. He sat there, listening, offering a comforting silence that somehow understood all of her struggles. And then he said, "Olivia, your passion for math shines through your eyes. But remember, we all have our unique rhythms. Your struggle isn't a failure; it's a testament to your courage in tackling something challenging."

He made her a promise – to break down those thorny concepts, to help her focus, and to reveal the creative spark within her. With his unwavering support, Olivia began to regain her footing. They spent countless hours together, brainstorming ideas, solving problems, and even delving into cosmic discussions about the universe's beauty and order. Olivia embraced Professor Graham's guidance and found a special connection with his focusing techniques. Sure, there were still those tough days when her old insecurities tried to creep back in. But now, she had a guiding light, someone reminding her that it's perfectly normal to struggle. Her academic journey was no straight path; it was a winding trail filled with ups and downs.

As she wrapped up her studies, Olivia had transformed into a confident math major, a person brimming with newfound resilience and a deep understanding of her abilities. She owed this transformation to Professor Graham, the mentor who had not only taught her to decode numbers but also helped her embrace her unique learning style.

Olivia's story illustrates the power of mentorship, turning struggles into strengths. It emphasizes the importance of compassion and understanding in the world of learning. Students are not empty vessels; they are brilliant minds waiting to be inspired and nurtured. If you find yourself facing similar academic challenges, remember Olivia's journey. Seek guidance, reach out to mentors or professors, and don't hesitate to ask for help. Embrace your unique learning style, and understand that difficulties are part of the learning process. With the right support and determination, you can transform your struggles into strengths, just like Olivia did.

College, with its blend of rigorous academics and personal growth, can challenge even the most independent souls. The next chapter will dive into the crucial skills you'll need to thrive, not just academically, but emotionally, mentally, and physically. Get ready to embark on this transformative journey!

Key Takeaways

- **Embrace Common Feelings:** It's normal to feel anxious and isolated when starting college, but remember, you're not alone—many students share these emotions.
- **Seek Connection:** Whether you're an introvert or extrovert, you can find connections through shared interests and mutual efforts. College is a place to form meaningful relationships.
- **Balance Solitude:** While solitude can be comforting, don't let it become isolating. Striking a balance between personal time and social

engagement is crucial for a fulfilling college experience.

- **Explore Opportunities:** College offers a wide range of group activities and hobbies. Don't hesitate to try new things, from sports to drama, to discover your passions and make friends who share your interests. College is a journey of self-discovery and connection —embrace it!

5 NAVIGATING COLLEGE WITH SPECIAL EDUCATION NEEDS

Embracing a New Chapter in Education

As you step into the exciting world of college, ready to embrace new experiences and broaden your horizons, it's essential to acknowledge that this transition may present unique challenges, particularly if you've navigated high school with special education needs. But the good news is, college can be a time of remarkable growth, empowerment, and achievement for you. This chapter is your guide to arming yourself with the tools, knowledge, and confidence to make your college journey not only successful but also incredibly fulfilling.

In high school, you may have benefited from a tailored support system that addressed your special education needs, including Individualized Education Programs (IEPs) and educators who understood your distinct learning style. As you venture into the college environment, which brings fresh experiences and a different approach to learning, it's natural to feel a bit overwhelmed initially. However, this transition also opens up a world of opportunities for further personal development, exploration of new interests, and the creation of a life that aligns with your dreams and capabilities.

College isn't just about academics; it's a voyage of self-discovery. As a student with special education needs, you'll become adept at advocating for yourself in ways you might not have explored before. You'll uncover your strengths, learn how to overcome challenges with resilience, and develop the determination to thrive.

In the pages that follow, we'll delve into understanding your rights as a college student with special education needs, getting ready for the transition, discovering and utilizing campus resources, and much more. Our aim is to equip you with the knowledge and strategies necessary to not only succeed but also excel in college, ensuring that your educational journey is both triumphant and enriching.

Always keep in mind that your college journey is uniquely yours. With the right resources and a proactive approach, you're not just destined to succeed; you're primed to shine.

Understanding Your Rights

Entering college means entering a new world of rights and responsibilities, especially for students with special education needs. It's crucial to understand that while college provides different protections than high school, you still have rights. Key among these are the Americans with Disabilities Act (ADA) and Section 504 of the Rehabilitation Act. These laws ensure that you have equal access to education and the right to reasonable accommodations for your learning needs.

The transition from high school to college is significant in terms of how these laws apply. In high school, under the Individuals with Disabilities Education Act (IDEA), you might have had an IEP that outlined specific services and support. In college, IDEA no longer applies, but the ADA and Section 504 do. This means that while colleges are required to provide accommodations, they are not required to identify you or design specialized programs. It's more about providing access and leveling the playing field.

This shift calls for a more proactive role in your education. You'll need to self-identify to your college's disability services office and possibly provide documentation of your disability. Remember, this is about ensuring that you receive the support you need, not about labeling you. It's a step toward independence and self-advocacy – key skills in college and beyond.

Preparing for the Transition

The move from high school to college is not just a physical one; it's a transition in mindset and approach. For students with special education needs, preparation is key. Start by understanding your learning style and the accommodations that have worked for you in the past. Self-awareness is a powerful tool in college.

Next, it's time to develop your self-advocacy skills. In college, you are your own best advocate. This means understanding your rights, knowing what accommodations you need, and being able to communicate these needs effectively to the right people. Practice expressing your needs clearly and confidently.

Also, consider creating an updated plan similar to your high school IEP for your personal use. While colleges don't follow IEPs, having a plan can help you articulate your needs and goals. This plan might include your learning strategies, potential accommodations, and who to contact for support.

Before the semester starts, reach out to your college's disability services office. They can guide you on the process of registering for accommodations, what documentation you'll need, and other services they offer. This is also a great time to connect with any student support groups or services that can aid your transition.

Remember, preparation for college is not just about academic readiness; it's also about being ready to take charge of your education and your needs. The more prepared you are, the smoother your transition to college will be.

Identifying College Resources

Once you're familiar with your rights and have begun preparing for the transition, the next step is to identify the resources available to you in college. Most colleges have a disability support services office (sometimes known by different names), which is your primary resource. This office can provide accommodations like note-taking services, extended time for exams, alternative exam locations, and assistive technology. They can also help you navigate the college environment, academically and socially.

But don't stop there. Explore other campus resources that can enhance your college experience. Libraries often have resources for students with learning differences, counseling centers can offer support for emotional challenges, and career services can assist with internships and job place-ments post-graduation. Remember, these services are there to help you succeed.

- **Document Instances:** Keep detailed records of instances when your accommodations are not met, including dates, specific classes, and descriptions of the situation. This can be important if you need to escalate the matter.
- **Re-Communicate with Disability Services:** If direct communication with the professor does not resolve the issue, revisit your college's disability support services. They can intervene and help clarify the

accommodations with your professor or the department.

- **Formal Grievance Procedure:** Most colleges have a formal grievance procedure for students to follow if their needs are not being met. If necessary, file a formal complaint. Your disability services office can guide you on how to proceed with this process.
- **Seek Support from Campus Advocacy Groups:** Many colleges have student advocacy groups or an ombudsman who can offer assistance and advice in resolving such issues. They can provide additional support and guidance on how to navigate these challenges.
- **Legal Action as a Last Resort:** If your accommodations are still not being met and you believe your rights under the ADA or Section 504 are being violated, consider seeking legal advice. Legal action is generally a last resort and should be pursued only after exhausting other avenues.

Remember, it's important to advocate for yourself and ensure that your educational needs are met. Your college is legally obligated to provide these

accommodations, and there are systems in place to support you in this process. Stay proactive, informed, and assertive about your needs, and don't hesitate to use the resources available to you for support and guidance.

Academic Support Services

Colleges typically offer academic support services that can be especially beneficial for students with special education needs. These services may include:

- **Disability Services Office:** Most colleges have a disability services office or a similar department. Contact this office as soon as possible to:
- Register your special education needs.
- Discuss and request accommodations tailored to your specific requirements, such as extended test-taking time, note-taking assistance, or accessible learning materials.
- Understand the documentation needed to verify your disability and eligibility for accommodations.
- **Academic Advising:** Your college's academic advising office can provide guidance on course selection, degree planning, and academic requirements. They can also help you align your academic goals with your individual learning needs.
- **Tutoring and Learning Centers:** Many colleges offer tutoring and learning centers that provide academic support. These centers can help you with coursework, study skills, and strategies for academic success.
- **Accessible Learning Materials:** Inquire about accessible learning materials, such as textbooks in alternative formats (e.g., audiobooks, digital texts, or

Braille) through your college's library or disability services office.

- **Mental Health and Counseling Services:** College life can be stressful, and it's essential to prioritize your mental health. Utilize on-campus counseling services to address emotional challenges and stress management.
- **Assistive Technology Labs:** Some colleges have assistive technology labs equipped with specialized software and hardware to assist students with disabilities. Explore these resources for assistive technologies that can aid in your studies.
- **Peer Mentorship Programs:** Check if your college offers peer mentorship programs. Connecting with a mentor who has experience navigating college with special education needs can provide valuable guidance and support.
- **Career Services:** As you progress through college, career services can assist you in exploring career options, building resumes, and preparing for job interviews, ensuring a smooth transition to the workforce.
- **Financial Aid Office:** Seek information on financial aid options and scholarships specifically designed for students with disabilities. These resources can help alleviate the financial burden of college.
- **Online Resources and Support Groups:** Explore online communities and support groups that cater to college students with special education needs.

These platforms can provide a sense of camaraderie and valuable advice.

- **Advocacy Groups:** Look for local or national advocacy groups that focus on the rights and support of students with disabilities. These organizations often offer resources and guidance on navigating college.
- **Campus Accessibility:** Familiarize yourself with the campus layout and accessibility features, such as accessible entrances, ramps, and designated parking spaces for students with disabilities.
- **Time Management Workshops:** Consider attending time management and study skills workshops offered by your college to improve your organizational and time management skills.

Key Takeaways

- **College Offers Growth and Success:** College is an opportunity for incredible personal growth, empowerment, and success, even if you've navigated high school with special education needs. Approach this new chapter with a positive outlook, knowing that you have the potential to thrive.
- **Understanding Your Rights:** While the transition from high school to college involves changes in how your rights are protected, remember that the Americans with Disabilities Act (ADA) and Section 504 of the Rehabilitation Act still ensure equal

access to education and reasonable accommodations.

- **Preparation and Self-Advocacy:** Prepare for the transition by understanding your learning style, developing self-advocacy skills, and creating a personalized plan that articulates your needs and goals. College requires a proactive approach to education and self-advocacy.

- **Identifying Resources:** Recognize the importance of identifying and utilizing college resources. Disability support services, academic advising, tutoring centers, counseling services, assistive technology labs, and more are available to help you succeed academically and personally.

- **Advocating for Your Needs:** Understand that advocating for your needs is essential. Keep records of any instances where your accommodations aren't met, communicate with professors and disability support services, and seek support from campus advocacy groups or legal action if necessary. Your education and rights matter, and there are avenues to ensure they are respected and upheld.

6 STRONGER, BETTER, FASTER

Strength does not come from winning. Your struggles develop your strengths. That is strength when you go through hardships and decide not to surrender. –Arnold Schwarzenegger

I n this chapter, you'll delve into actionable strategies aimed at cultivating mental serenity. These approaches will empower you to effectively cope with stress and anxiety, bolster your resilience, nurture a sense of independence and responsibility, and embrace mindful self-care routines. The ultimate aim is to assist you in crafting a well-rounded and satisfying student life.

Why Is College So Emotionally Challenging?

College is a step up from high school, presenting more substantial and diverse academic demands. Here, you're not just a student; you're the captain of your educational voyage. The pressure to navigate these challenging waters brews a potent stress cocktail, often leading to overwhelming anxiety and depression.

A Fear That Looms Large

The fear of failure extends beyond academics and permeates your broader college experience. It's a phase where you're sculpting your identity and making life-altering decisions. The weight of societal, familial, and self-imposed expectations can fuel a constant sense of stress and anxiety. The fear of making wrong choices and falling short of those expectations can be suffocating.

Navigating the Social Maze

Building new friendships, assimilating into social circles, and nurturing relationships can be emotionally taxing. For many, bonding with others isn't effortless, resulting in feelings of isolation and loneliness. Leaving behind the familiar faces of home further intensifies this sense of solitude. College often marks the first step into independent life, making the absence of a familiar support system palpable. The transition from adolescence to adulthood involves continual change, testing your resilience in a whirlwind of new environments and responsibilities.

The Weight of Financial Stress

The towering costs of tuition, accommodation, textbooks, and daily expenses can trigger financial anxiety. Many students opt for part-time jobs, adding to an already substantial workload. Balancing work and studies can blur your focus, hindering both academic and personal growth.

The Neglected Basics

Neglecting rest, maintaining an unbalanced diet, shunning exercise, and indulging in unhealthy habits like excessive alcohol consumption can wreak havoc on your physical and emotional well-being. These often-overlooked factors can significantly contribute to feelings of anxiety and depression.

The Digital Dilemma

While technology connects us, the burden of maintaining an online presence can add to your troubles. Social media can act as a double-edged sword, fueling feelings of inadequacy and loneliness when comparing your life to curated narratives. The pressure to project a picture-perfect life online can lead to a disconcerting disconnect from reality, intensifying emotional distress.

Guiding Light of Assistance

Amid these challenges, educational institutions play a crucial role. They must acknowledge the storms you face and provide support through counseling, stress management workshops, and fostering a supportive community. By promoting a balanced approach to work and life, they pave the way for a nurturing environment conducive to both academic and personal growth.

Navigating the Emotional Storm

Emotional challenges in college are complex and inter-twined. Academic pressures, social dynamics, personal development, fear of failure, financial burdens, health concerns, and the digital landscape together create a challenging backdrop that can lead to anxiety, depression, and loneliness. Yet, with guidance from educational institutions, friends, and family, you can overcome these obstacles and make the most of this invaluable phase of life. Acknowledging and addressing these emotional challenges is key to emerging as confident, resilient, and emotionally healthy individuals.

Reframing Negative or Unhelpful Thoughts

In the grand theater of life, it's not uncommon to find yourself caught in the gusts of harmful self-talk – those subtle whispers that cast shadows on your spirit, sow seeds of self-doubt, and shackle your boundless potential. These thoughts create a canvas of despair, echoing phrases like "Can I really handle this test?" "Do I fit in here, or am I like the odd one out?" or "Have I turned into an expert at messing things up (and not the fun kind)?" Yet, these are nothing more than treacherous illusions woven from distortions, exaggerations, or unfounded assumptions, devoid of a solid footing in facts or evidence.

- In this chapter, we're diving into a journey that can change the way you think. You'll discover how to recognize, understand, and turn those harmful thoughts into positive ones that can make your life better. This shift in perspective can help reduce stress, anxiety, and sadness, boost your self-confidence, ignite your motivation, and bring more happiness into your life.

- You might be wondering how to start this process. Well, we've got a bunch of steps and strategies to help you out. As we go through this chapter, we'll reveal the secrets of becoming a master at turning negative or unhelpful thoughts into something better. So, get ready to upgrade your mental toolbox and join us on this enlightening adventure!

Cultivate Thought Awareness

Foster Thought Awareness: Your initial objective is to develop the skill of recognizing these detrimental whispers and understanding their origins. Utilize mindfulness techniques to observe your thoughts, emotions, and sensations in the present moment without judgment. This practice enables you to delve into your thought patterns and their impact on your well-being. Alternatively, maintaining a journal or notebook can help externalize your thoughts, providing you with a more objective view of your inner world.

By consistently engaging in these practices, you'll gain deeper insights into your thought processes, recognizing recurring patterns and triggers that lead to unhelpful or negative thinking. Moreover, you'll uncover the connection between your thoughts and your emotional state, offering valuable information to reshape your perspective.

Keep in mind that cultivating thought awareness is a gradual process. Patience is key as you allow the practice to unfold naturally. With each step, you'll become better equipped to navigate your thoughts and transform them into tools for personal growth and mental resilience.

Subject Your Thoughts to Scrutiny

Now, let's move on to the next phase where you'll put your thoughts through a thorough examination, scrutinizing their validity and usefulness. Here's how you can approach it:

- **Question their Validity:** Begin by asking if your thought is grounded in reality. Challenge it by seeking concrete evidence to either support or refute it. This step helps you discern whether your thought is based on facts or unfounded assumptions.

- **Assess their Utility:** Evaluate whether the thought is constructive or destructive. Consider how it affects your emotions and behaviors. Does it empower you, or does it drag you down? Understanding the impact of your thoughts is crucial for reshaping your mindset.

- **Identify Cognitive Distortions:** Recognize any cognitive distortions that might be influencing your thoughts. These distortions can include magnification (making issues seem larger than they are), overgeneralization (drawing broad conclusions from limited experiences), or black-and-white thinking (seeing things as all good or all bad).

- **Examine Consequences:** Think about the potential consequences of embracing this thought. How might it impact your decisions, relationships, or well-being? Understanding the potential fallout can motivate you to adopt a more constructive perspective.

By subjecting your thoughts to this critical examination, you'll gain a deeper understanding of their nature and how they shape your perception of reality. This self-awareness is a crucial step towards reframing negative or unhelpful thoughts, allowing you to make conscious choices about the beliefs you hold and the impact they have on your life. Remember, this process takes time and practice, so be patient with yourself as you work towards reshaping your thought patterns.

Craft Positive Alternatives

Now, let's delve into your third mission, which is all about cultivating positive and constructive thought patterns. Here are some effective techniques to help you reshape your thoughts:

- **Socratic Questioning:** Challenge negative thoughts by asking yourself probing questions. Encourage critical thinking by inquiring about the evidence behind your thoughts, their validity, and alternative perspectives. This method helps you gain clarity and develop a more balanced view.

- **Guided Imagery:** Visualize positive outcomes and scenarios. When you catch yourself in a negative thought loop, redirect your imagination toward more optimistic possibilities. Visualization can shift your mindset and boost your confidence.

- **Positive Reframing:** Train your mind to find the silver lining in challenging situations. Instead of dwelling on the negatives, focus on the potential lessons, growth opportunities, or hidden advantages. This approach can transform setbacks into stepping stones.

- **Depersonalization:** Detach yourself from your thoughts by viewing them as passing mental events rather than absolute truths. Understand that thoughts are not facts, and they do not define your identity or worth.

- **Growth Mindset:** Embrace the belief that you can learn and grow from experiences, challenges, and failures. Cultivate a mindset that sees setbacks as opportunities for development rather than as reflections of your capabilities.

- **Positive Self-Talk:** Counteract negative thoughts with encouraging and compassionate self-talk. Replace self-criticism with self-affirmation, and remind yourself of your strengths and achievements.

By employing these techniques consistently, you can gradually shift your thought patterns towards positivity and resilience. It's important to remember that reframing negative thoughts is an ongoing process that requires practice. Be patient with yourself and celebrate your progress along the way. As you become more adept at crafting positive alternatives, you'll enhance your mental resilience and overall well-being.

Consistency Is Key

Your final task centers around the ongoing practice of this cycle—observing and reshaping your thoughts until they transform into dependable allies. Utilize reminders such as sticky notes, alarms, or dedicated apps to prompt mindfulness at various points throughout the day. Celebrate your achievements and commemorate the victories, no matter how small they may seem.

As you continue on this journey of self-transformation, you'll gradually free yourself from the clutches of harmful self-talk. Instead, you'll embark on a path of empowerment and self-discovery, fostering a mindset that bolsters your mental resilience and fuels your personal growth.

Remember that personal growth is an evolving process, and each step you take brings you closer to becoming the best version of yourself. Embrace the power of thought awareness and transformation, and watch as it unfolds in every aspect of your life, enhancing your overall well-being and resilience.

Your Biology = Your Psychology

College life can be demanding, affecting both your physical and mental well-being. To navigate this journey successfully, consider the following:

Prioritize Rest:

- Aim for 7-9 hours of quality sleep each night.
- Establish a consistent sleep schedule.
- Embrace Nourishment:
- Choose nutrient-rich meals to enhance mood and cognitive function.
- Limit fast food and sugar consumption.

Stay Active:

- Engage in physical activities you enjoy for at least 150 minutes per week.
- Cultivate Mindfulness and Stillness:
- Incorporate mindfulness practices, such as meditation or yoga, into your routine.
- Find moments of calm amid the college chaos.

Efficient Time Management:

- Create a well-structured schedule to balance academic tasks and self-care.
- Include self-care breaks within your schedule.

Embrace Your Community:

- Spend quality time with friends and family for emotional support.
- Consider study groups for collaborative learning.

Utilize Campus Resources:

- Access counseling services for emotional well-being.
- Explore fitness facilities and classes on campus.
- Make healthy food choices available on campus.

Personal Time and Enjoyment:

- Pursue hobbies and interests outside of academics.
- Practice self-reflection and journaling.

Financial Wellness:

- Create a budget and stick to it to alleviate financial stress.
- Seek financial guidance if needed.

By prioritizing these aspects, you can maintain the balance between your mental and physical health and make the most of your college experience.

Key Takeaways

- **Understanding College's Emotional Challenges:** College presents substantial academic demands, coupled with the pressure of shaping your identity and making crucial life decisions. Recognize that stress and anxiety are common, stemming from academic, social, financial, and personal pressures.
- **Recognizing Harmful Thought Patterns:** Learn to identify and challenge negative or unhelpful thoughts that can contribute to stress, anxiety, and depression. These thoughts are often distortions or exaggerations lacking factual basis.
- **Developing Thought Awareness:** Cultivate the skill of thought awareness through mindfulness techniques and journaling. This practice allows you to recognize recurring patterns and triggers that lead to unhelpful thinking.
- **Subjecting Thoughts to Scrutiny:** Examine your thoughts for validity and utility. Question whether they are based on reality, assess their impact on your emotions and behaviors, identify cognitive distortions, and evaluate potential consequences.
- **Crafting Positive Alternatives:** Implement techniques like Socratic questioning, guided imagery, positive reframing, and positive self-talk to reshape negative thoughts into constructive ones. This shift in perspective can reduce stress, boost self-confidence, and promote overall well-being.

7 WORK-SCHOOL-LIFE BALANCE

Happiness is not a matter of intensity but of balance,
order, rhythm, and harmony. –Thomas Merton

Meet Brittany

Meet Brittany, a college student juggling classes, a part-time job, and helping her mom due to her health issues. Balancing everything can be overwhelming.

To stay on track, Brittany's become a scheduling pro, blocking out time for her responsibilities. She also practices quick stress-relief techniques, like meditation and short walks in the campus park.

But the pressure can still build up. After a tough exam, Brittany reached out to a college counselor who suggested she join a support group for students dealing with similar challenges.

Being part of that group made a big difference. Brittany realized it's okay to ask for help when needed. She's found her rhythm and knows that with smart planning, mindfulness, and the courage to seek assistance, she can handle college while caring for herself and her family.

The Working Student's Adventure

Now, let's introduce Liam Thompson, a bright-eyed freshman from a small coastal town who found himself navigating the overwhelming maze of university life in the big city. His dorm room resembled a cramped library, filled with books and mementos from home.

Liam worked at an old-fashioned bookstore, a treasure trove of aging paper and shelves filled with wisdom. His boss, Mr. Jennings, was kind but stern, valuing Liam's strong work ethic. Classes were a mix of excitement and stress, yet Dr. Hughes, a passionate history professor, recognized Liam's potential and fatigue. Their coffee-fueled conversations became Liam's guiding light, helping him navigate the delicate balance of work, studies, and life.

Slowly, Liam's world expanded. He made friends, explored hidden city alleys, and even dipped his toes into the world of dating. The bookstore's regular customers transformed into familiar faces, exchanging stories and wisdom.

As his grades improved, so did his quality of life. The once-daunting juggling act of work and study evolved into a well-coordinated dance. When Liam donned his graduation cap, Mr. Jennings beamed proudly from the audience. Liam's journey wasn't just about earning a degree; it was about personal growth, resilience, and the rich tapestry of connections he had woven along the way.

Balance On the Tightrope

College is a bustling marketplace brimming with opportunities to explore your passions, interests, and hobbies. Whether you join a club, engage in sports, or volunteer, these pursuits do more than just bring joy—they weave connections and enrich your college journey. Yet, amidst the vibrancy, stress often looms nearby, casting shadows of immense pressure, sleepless nights, and anxious days.

But fret not, for you possess powerful tools to shield yourself. The practices of mindfulness, positive thinking, and seeking professional guidance can serve as your protective armor. Admittedly, the path isn't always smooth. At times, you may stumble, unintentionally neglecting facets of your life due to time constraints or waning motivation. It's akin to forgetting to water a plant, which may manifest as a dip in academic performance or a dwindling sense of happiness.

Neglecting areas such as sleep or social interaction can deplete your energy, fostering feelings of isolation or unhappiness. Worse still, it may lead to a decline in mental well-being, with unhealthy coping mechanisms taking a toll on your health.

So, what's the key to navigating this intricate balancing act? It's about finding a unique equilibrium, like adjusting the sails on a boat to ensure smooth passage. Nurturing all aspects of your life is the compass that guides you to better grades, a happier heart, reduced stress, and a truly fulfilling college experience. Remember, the perfect balance isn't discovered; it's meticulously crafted with care, attention, and a deep understanding of oneself.

Avoiding Overcommitment: Finding the Right Balance

The Excitement-Overload Dilemma

Entering college as a freshman brings with it a sense of excitement and a world of opportunities. You're eager to explore new subjects, make friends, and maybe even take on a part-time job or join various extracurricular activities. While enthusiasm and a willingness to embrace new experiences are admirable qualities, it's crucial to strike a balance to avoid falling into the trap of overcommitment.

The Overcommitment Pitfall

Overcommitment occurs when you take on more responsibilities and commitments than you can realistically manage. It often stems from the desire to excel academically, build a strong resume, or simply fear of missing out on valuable experiences. However, overcommitting can lead to excessive stress, burnout, and negatively impact both your academic performance and overall well-being.

Recognizing the Signs

It's essential to recognize the signs of overcommitment early on to prevent it from taking a toll on your college experience. Here are some common indicators:

- **Feeling Overwhelmed:** If you constantly feel overwhelmed, unable to catch your breath, or find it challenging to keep up with your obligations, it's a clear sign you might be overcommitted.
- **Decline in Academic Performance:** A significant drop in your grades or difficulty in managing your coursework can be a result of spreading yourself too thin.
- **Lack of Sleep and Exhaustion:** Consistently staying up late to meet deadlines or feeling exhausted even after a full night's sleep can be indicators of overcommitment.
- **Neglecting Self-Care:** When you no longer have time for self-care activities like exercise, hobbies, or spending time with friends and family, it's a red flag.
- **Increased Irritability:** If you find yourself becoming easily irritated or losing patience with others, it might be due to the stress of overcommitment.

Strategies to Avoid Overcommitment

Now that you understand the risks of overcommitment, let's explore strategies to help you maintain a healthy balance:

- **Prioritize Your Commitments:** Identify your most important commitments, whether they are academic, work-related, or extracurricular. Focus on these and be selective about additional responsibilities.
- **Create a Schedule:** Develop a realistic daily and weekly schedule that includes dedicated time for studying, work, relaxation, and social activities.
- **Set Boundaries:** Learn to say no when necessary. It's okay to decline additional tasks or commitments if you're already stretched thin.
- **Seek Support:** Reach out to academic advisors, professors, or mentors for guidance in managing your academic workload and extracurricular activities.
- **Time Management:** Improve your time management skills by setting specific goals, breaking tasks into smaller steps, and using tools like planners or digital calendars.
- **Evaluate Your Goals:** Periodically review your goals and commitments. Consider whether they still align with your long-term objectives and make adjustments as needed.

- **Balance Self-Care:** Prioritize self-care activities, including exercise, relaxation, and spending time with loved ones. These activities help recharge your energy and reduce stress.
- **Seek Help When Needed:** If you find yourself consistently overwhelmed, don't hesitate to seek support from counseling services or student support groups on campus.

Freshman year is a time of exploration, growth, and self-discovery. While the excitement of new opportunities is thrilling, it's vital to strike a balance between your responsibilities. Recognizing the signs of overcommitment and implementing strategies to maintain a healthy balance will not only enhance your college experience but also set you on a path to personal and academic success. Remember, your journey through college is uniquely yours, and finding that perfect equilibrium is a valuable skill you'll carry with you throughout your academic and personal life.

Effective Communication: Your Ticket to Success

Welcome to the realm of academia and work, where you find yourself at a crossroads armed with your thoughts, ideas, feelings, and the words you choose to convey them. As a student managing the weight of studies and potentially a job, mastering the art of communication will be your compass through both challenges and triumphs.

Act One: Building Blocks of Communication

Communication skills are like the building blocks of a cool castle. It's all about listening, talking, writing, reading, and picking up on those nonverbal signals. Imagine being an eagle-eyed listener, a smooth-talking speaker, and a writing pro. When you master these skills, you not only boost yourself but also make things clearer for everyone around you, avoiding those awkward conflicts.

Act Two: Critical Thinking and Problem-Solving Skills

Next up, we've got critical thinking and problem-solving skills on the agenda. Picture yourself as a crafty problem solver, taking raw challenges and hammering out solutions with logic. It's all about learning to express your ideas in a convincing and creative way. When you can assess info, back up your arguments with evidence, and tailor your message for different folks, you become a super adaptable and sharp communicator.

Final Act: Open and Honest Communication

Now, let's talk about open and honest communication when it comes to your expectations and needs. Think of it as your growth garden. You're the gardener here, making sure your communication flowers and thrives with transparency and sincerity. As a student, you've got to be on top of it, chatting with your teachers, classmates, or bosses about your goals, challenges, and what you need. Don't be shy to ask for help, give some feedback, say thanks, or talk through your needs – it's like a cool breeze blowing success your way.

When the curtains close, you'll retain not just a skill but an art, a guiding force, and a companion in effective communication. You hold the palette and brushes to paint your academic and professional life with vibrant colors of understanding, collaboration, stress management, and enhanced performance. Embrace these principles and skills, and witness the world around you transform into a canvas of boundless possibilities.

Key Takeaways

- **Balancing Act:** Brittany, the college student, shows us that balancing academics, a part-time job, and family responsibilities can be overwhelming. To stay on track, Brittany excels at scheduling and practices stress-relief techniques like meditation and short walks. Seeking help when needed and joining a support group can make a big difference in managing life's challenges.
- **Liam's Journey:** Liam's story highlights a student's adventure in balancing work, life, and studies. With resilience and the support of mentors and friends, Liam navigated the challenges of university life, expanding his world along the way. His journey reminds us that personal growth and connections are integral to the college experience.
- **Balance on the Tightrope:** College life offers numerous opportunities, but it can also bring stress and pressure. Mindfulness, positive thinking, and

seeking professional guidance are powerful tools to manage these challenges. Finding a unique equilibrium, nurturing all aspects of your life, and avoiding neglecting areas like sleep and social interaction are essential for a fulfilling college experience.

8 OUT OF THE NEST

T *he bond that links your true family is not one of blood but of respect and joy in each other's life.* –Richard Bach

Imagine yourself in your brand-new kitchen. It might be cozy, but it's entirely yours. The thrill of not having to rely on takeout or your parents' cooking fills you with joy. Learning to cook isn't just about satisfying your hunger; it's a symbol of independence, a delightful marker of growing up. And guess what? It can be as straightforward as mastering a favorite pasta recipe that not only saves you money but tastes exactly the way you love it.

Now, consider these life skills that extend beyond the kitchen —budgeting, cleaning, fixing a leaky faucet. While they may seem mundane, they are the stepping stones to self-sufficiency. You'll no longer have to call someone else to handle these tasks. You become the hero of your own home, conquering daily life like a pro.

But adulthood isn't solely about self-reliance; it's about building connections too. You'll need to communicate, negotiate, and sometimes even engage in disagreements. However, with the right attitude and determination, you'll form friendships, partnerships, and maybe even discover a love connection or two. It's all part of the exhilarating journey of self-discovery and understanding what you want from life. You might also embark on a new job or academic journey, further expanding your horizons. The ability to network, craft an impressive resume, or ace an interview isn't just about advancing your career; it's a means of personal growth. You're shaping your future with every email sent, hand shaken, and success celebrated.

Undoubtedly, adulting can be challenging, but it's also incredibly thrilling and fulfilling. Remember, you're not alone on this adventure. With each step, you'll uncover more of yourself and your true capabilities. Embrace the beauty of becoming an adult; it's a journey worth savoring.

The Parent Trap

Navigating the evolving dynamics with your parents is pivotal during this transitional phase. Once your primary caregivers and mentors, they now find themselves grappling with the idea of loosening the reins. This shift can sometimes lead to tension and conflicts as they struggle to let go of control, a process often marked by resistance. Why does this struggle persist? The reasons are multifaceted:

- **Invested Support:** Parents have dedicated significant time, energy, and resources to nurture your success. Their pride in your achievements coexists with anxiety about the future, along with the fear of losing the close connection and influence they've had as you venture into independence.
- **Entrenched Parenting Habits:** Habits and routines associated with parenting are deeply ingrained. Whether it's checking your homework or participating in decision-making, their involvement in various aspects of your life has become second nature. Shifting toward a less controlling relationship can indeed be challenging.
- **Shifting Expectations:** Sometimes, expectations parents have regarding your college experience may not align with your reality or desires. Whether it's the desire for you to follow in their footsteps, share their values and goals, or chart a specific path, they may grapple with reconciling their aspirations with your unique journey.

Growing Up and Moving On

Responsibility is a badge of honor that we should proudly wear, not something to lament. It may not always be visible, but it shines through our actions in various ways. One of its first gleams is found in keeping promises. When you make a commitment, it's essential to follow through. This consistency allows people to place their trust in you, akin to a steadfast bridge enduring even the fiercest storms.

Time management is another facet of responsibility. Respecting your own time, as well as others', is significant. Being punctual for meetings, dates, or events conveys a message of respect and seriousness, saying, "I value you, and I take our engagements seriously."

Financial responsibility is yet another indicator of maturity. It's not about having vast wealth; it's about using your resources wisely. In today's uncertain world, financial stability can provide a sense of security and hope. When you make a mistake, taking responsibility and owning up to it is essential. Blaming others may be the easy way out, but acknowledging your errors requires courage and maturity. Being proactive is also a demonstration of responsibility. It means not waiting passively but taking the lead, investing effort, and actively participating in tasks and endeavors.

The Unbroken Threads

Let's talk about Jane and her dad, Tom. Growing up, Jane was her father Tom's most cherished treasure. As she prepared to embark on her journey into college life, leaving behind her small-town roots, Tom was filled with pride, but beneath that, a nagging fear loomed. It wasn't just the typical separation anxiety; it was the fear of an uncertain future he couldn't control or shield her from.

During her initial weeks at college, Jane found herself in a whirlwind of new faces, friendships, and newfound freedoms. Tom's calls were met with quick reassurances like, "I'm good, Dad. Gotta run!" But these rushed responses left Tom feeling uneasy. He was worried about his daughter's well-being and couldn't help but wonder what she was up to, who she was spending time with, and if she was safe.

For Jane, college was a chance to express her individuality, and she saw her father's concerns as nothing more than restrictions. She felt like he was questioning her integrity, which led to arguments and misunderstandings. Tom's wife, Maria, saw the growing divide between them and empathized with Tom's anxiety while understanding Jane's desire for independence. Despite their efforts to bridge the gap, Jane's resistance only grew stronger. Over time, their once-strong connection dwindled, replaced by anger and silence.

As Jane stopped confiding in her parents, her academic performance suffered, and she made misguided decisions, all in the name of autonomy. When summer finally arrived, Jane returned home a shadow of her former self. During a family dinner, emotions overflowed. Jane's composed exterior crumbled, revealing her insecurities and need for guidance. Tom, equally moved, shared his fears and his desire to protect her, realizing that he needed to let go of control.

Their heartfelt exchange marked a new beginning. Together, they worked to rebuild their bond, a slow process filled with understanding and acceptance of each other's imperfections. By the time Jane's second year of college began, they had found a balance between independence and guidance. Tom recognized Jane's maturity, and Jane understood that growing older didn't mean growing apart. Their college years became a time of growth not only for Jane but also for Tom. They both learned that faith, communication, and empathy were crucial in preserving their connection. They had to evolve, mature, and transform to find their way back to each other.

Through it all, they realized that the love between a parent and child could endure, adapt, and flourish, even in the face of fears, misunderstandings, and immaturity. This understanding became a symbol of their unbreakable bond.

Maintaining a Supportive and Connected Relationship

As the holiday season approaches, college students, now seasoned with newfound independence, prepare to return home. It's a time to embrace the familial warmth, relish in the nostalgia of home-cooked meals, and find solace in the familiarity of one's surroundings. Yet, this homecoming is also a delicate balancing act, a dance between the autonomy cultivated during campus life and the shared expectations of being back home. In this intricate tango, two key components come into play: setting boundaries and distributing household responsibilities. Let's delve into the heart of these matters.

Ground Rules: Building the Pillars of Mutual Respect

The academic world grants students the freedom to foster personal growth and independence. It's a time when you learn to live life on your terms, and sometimes, these newfound ways of living don't seamlessly align with your family's home environment. Unsurprisingly, returning home can lead to some friction, akin to a cultural shock.

To preempt potential conflicts, it's crucial to initiate clear communication regarding expectations and boundaries right from the start. This dialogue should be an opportunity to respect and consider both your perspectives and your parents'. Topics may encompass curfews, visitors, personal space, and even culinary preferences.

It's equally important to encourage a two-way understanding. While your parents may have concerns about certain aspects of your behavior, you also have the right to express your evolved lifestyle and thought processes. The aim is to reach a mutual understanding and, when necessary, find a middle ground that respects your identity as a college student while honoring your family's values.

Domestic Duties

Transitioning from the relatively relaxed atmosphere of college life to the more structured home environment often raises questions about household responsibilities. Who is responsible for what? Are college students expected to participate in household chores, and if so, to what extent?

To set clear expectations, open dialogue once again plays a crucial role. It's essential for you and your parents to have discussions about the division of household tasks, including cooking, cleaning, and taking care of younger siblings or pets.

Finding the right balance is key. While it's reasonable to expect your contribution to household chores, recognizing your unique circumstances may require some flexibility. For instance, if you're returning home to study or work part-time, adjusting the chore schedule could be beneficial.

Engaging in household tasks should not be seen as an imposition. Instead, consider it an opportunity to make a positive contribution to the family and strengthen your bonds. It allows your parents to witness your growth, and in turn, you can contribute to enhancing the family dynamic.

Additional Items When Navigating Transitions Between College and Home:

Shifting between college life and returning home during breaks can be a bit of a rollercoaster. You might experience what's called "reverse culture shock" as you adapt to being back in your hometown. To help smooth out this adjustment:

Keep the Lines of Communication Open:

Staying connected with your family is key. Share your college experiences and the changes you've gone through while listening to their stories too. It can make the transition back home much smoother.

Coping with Change:

Change is a constant in life, and moving towards adulthood and independence can be a real challenge, both for you and your parents. Here's how to navigate this period of change:

Patience and Understanding:

Be patient with yourself and your family as everyone adapts to new roles and dynamics. Understand that change can be uncertain, but it's also an opportunity for growth and development.

Taking Care of Your Mental Health:

Your mental health is super important during this time. College can bring on stress and anxiety, so here's what you should know:

Seek Support: Don't hesitate to reach out for support when needed. Your college probably offers mental health resources, and there are local services at home too. Never forget to prioritize your mental well-being.

Being Money-Savvy:

Let's talk finances! Managing your money is a crucial part of growing up. Here's what you need to know:

Budgeting: Learn the ropes of budgeting. Create a monthly budget to keep track of your income and expenses. It's a great way to manage your finances responsibly.

Open Talks About Money: Have honest conversations with your parents about financial matters. Discuss your financial responsibilities and how you can help with expenses at home. It's all about being open and transparent.

Resolving Conflicts:

Conflicts can happen; it's a part of life. Here's how to deal with them effectively:

Effective Communication: Practice good communication skills. Listen actively, express your thoughts and feelings respectfully, and aim to understand each other's perspectives. Finding common ground can help resolve disagreements.

Setting Your Goals:

Setting goals, both personal and academic, is a fantastic habit. Here's why:

Personal Growth: Goal-setting is all about personal growth and success. During college breaks, set clear goals for yourself to stay motivated and focused. These goals can cover everything from your studies to your personal development.

Seeking Guidance:

Don't hesitate to reach out for help and guidance during your college years:

Connect with Mentors: Professors, advisors, and counselors are here to support you. Reach out to them for advice as you navigate your academic and personal journey. Building these relationships can be incredibly helpful.

The Role of Siblings:

If you have siblings, they're a part of your family dynamic too:

Understanding Siblings: Your siblings might also be adjusting to your presence at home. Try to understand their perspective and feelings during this transition. Open and empathetic communication can strengthen your relationship with them.

Building Resilience:

Challenges and change can make you stronger:

Embrace Challenges: Face challenges as opportunities for growth. Overcoming obstacles during your college years will build resilience and prepare you for the future. Remember, you're more capable than you might think.

The Power of Self-Reflection:

Self-reflection is a super useful tool:

Self-Assessment: Engage in self-reflection activities like journaling or self-assessment exercises. These practices can help you gain insights into your personal growth and development. It's a great way to make the most of your college experience and transitions.

These tips and insights are here to help you navigate the exciting but sometimes tricky journey of college life and beyond. If you ever need more guidance or have specific questions, feel free to ask. Your journey is worth savoring and making the most of!

Key Takeaways

- Stepping over the threshold from youth into adulthood, you face a kaleidoscope of challenges and treasures. Think of it as a mystery box—brimming with lessons in life skills such as whipping up a meal, budgeting wisely, and ensuring your home doesn't crumble into disarray. You're also met with fresh responsibilities, such as starting your first job or immersing yourself in the buzz of university life.
- Drawing from the narrative of Jane and her father, Tom, the text spotlights the pivotal role communication and understanding play in parent-child relationships. Misinterpretations and roadblocks in communication can create fissures, affecting trust, academic prowess, and mental wellness. Open dialogue and a healthy dose of empathy form the cornerstone of healing and growth.

AFTERWORD

As we reach the conclusion of this book, it becomes abundantly clear that college is not merely a stepping stone to the "real world." It's a vibrant and transformative world of its own, filled with a myriad of opportunities, friendships, triumphs, failures, laughter, and tears. Above all, it's a realm of immense personal growth.

Picture this: You are now standing at the threshold of an exciting new chapter where classrooms transcend mere textbooks and lectures. They become arenas of debate, innovation, and discovery. Your professors are not just instructors; they can be your mentors, guiding you on your quest for knowledge. While navigating the academic landscape is a significant part of your college journey, it's only one piece of the puzzle.

Throughout your college experience, you'll discover joy in extracurricular activities, resilience during late-night cramming sessions, and tenacity in coffee-fueled morning classes. Undoubtedly, you'll face challenges, from financial constraints to overwhelming stress. These challenges, however, are not mere obstacles; they are catalysts that will shape you into a stronger, more compassionate individual.

But here's the secret to thriving in college – you are never alone on this adventure. Reach out for help when needed, whether it's leaning on your friends, seeking guidance from professors, or utilizing counseling services. Your college community is there to support you through every trial and triumph.

In addition to overcoming challenges, don't forget to have fun. Explore new hobbies, attend campus events, join clubs and societies, and dance like no one's watching at college festivals. College is a time of self-discovery, and embracing every facet of it, from academics to extracurriculars, is key to your personal growth.

So, as we raise a toast to your college years, remember this: Be bold, be inquisitive, and, above all, be yourself. Approach college with an open heart, a curious mind, and an eagerness to grow. This is your story to write, so make it a masterpiece! Your college journey is an incredible adventure, and you have all the tools you need to make it a truly remarkable chapter in your life. Cheers to the exciting journey ahead!

BIBLIOGRAPHY

- Arnold Schwarzenegger Quotes. (n.d.). BrainyQuote. https://www.brainyquote.com/quotes/arnold_schwarzenegger_116694
- Boogaard, K. (2021, December 26). How to write SMART goals. https://www.atlassian.com/blog/productivity/how-to-write-smart-goals#:~:text=What%20are%20SMART%20-goals%3F,within%20a%20certain%
- 20time%20frame.
- Duncan, A. (2013, April 23). Education: The most powerful weapon for changing the world. USAID. https://blog.usaid.-gov/2013/04/education-the-most-powerful-weapon/
- Misty Copeland quotes. (n.d.). BrainyQuote. https://www.brainyquote.com/quotes/misty_copeland_749724 More than 50% of gen z college students report feeling lonely according to sodexo student lifestyle survey. (2022, August 9). Sodexo. https://us.sodexo.com/media/news-releases/gen-z-college-students-lonely.html
- Rainer Maria Rilke quotes. (n.d.). BrainyQuote. https://www.brainyquote.com/quotes/rainer_maria_rilke_147758
- Richard Bach quotes. (n.d.). BrainyQuote. https://www.brainyquote.com/quotes/richard_bach_134891
- Socrates quotes. (n.d.). BrainyQuote. https://www.brainyquote.com/quotes/socrates_101212
- The reflection of education that you can use to change the world. (n.d.). 123HelpMe.https://www.123helpme.com/essay/The-Reflection-Of-Education-That-You-

CanFC6A69UD26#:~:text=%E2%80%9CEduca-
tion%20is%20the%20most%20powerful,
(Martin%20Luther%20King%20Jr).

- 31 alarming college student mental health statistics. (2022, August
  2). What to Become. https://whattobecome.com/blog/college-
  student-mental-health-statistics/
- Thomas Merton quotes. (n.d.). BrainyQuote.
  https://www.brainyquote.com/quotes/thomas_merton_385072

LIFE SKILLS 101:

THE CRASH COURSE IN ADULTING - BECAUSE APPARENTLY YOU SHOULD KNOW THIS BY NOW

INTRODUCTION

"Success is not final, failure is not fatal: It is the courage to continue that counts." - Winston Churchill

---

Ever feel like adulting is a wild rollercoaster ride with no seatbelts? Welcome to the not-so-secret club of young adulthood! Life's a blend of epic adventures and bewildering mazes. But fear not, this guide is your treasure map, helping you navigate health, wealth, relationships, and self-care like a pro. Get ready to conquer the adulting maze with style!

Think of this guide as a friendly chat about everything you're supposed to know as an adult but maybe no one thought to teach you along the way. We're talking about the nitty-gritty of managing healthcare – that includes understanding appropriate social etiquette especially in group settings or traveling. These are situations you are less likely to have encountered while in high school. And then there's the whole world of learning how to manage your finances to be prepared for whatever situation that life will put you in. We've got you.

But it's not all paperwork and health jargon. Life's also about the connections you make and the relationships you build. This book dives into the art of safely dating (offline and online), maintaining healthy relationships, and even getting a grip on sexual health education – because it's a big part of life.

And then there's money – the root of so much adulting stress. We'll walk you through budgeting, managing your finances, and even the ins and outs of side hustles. Because who doesn't want a little extra cash?

Living on your own is another big leap. Whether finding your place, whipping up a decent meal, or figuring out how to do laundry without calling home, we cover the essentials of independent living. And let's not forget about the digital world we're living in. Your online life, from social media to digital literacy, is as real as your offline one. Navigating it safely and smartly is key.

Most importantly, we're here to talk about mental health and well-being. Taking care of your mind is as important as caring for your body. Understanding mental health, developing coping strategies, and knowing when and how to seek help is vital.

This guide is about getting you equipped with the skills and knowledge to live your best life. It's casual, straightforward, and hopefully, a bit fun. So, let's dive into these pages and uncover the secrets to navigating your early twenties with confidence and a bit of flair.

1 HEALTHCARE 101

Ever wondered why adulting doesn't come with an instruction manual? Well, here's a question for you: Do you know how to navigate the healthcare maze as a savvy consumer? This chapter is your backstage pass to understanding the ins and outs of healthcare in the real world, where you're not just the patient but also the decision-maker. As you navigate the exciting path of independence, you might encounter various healthcare challenges, from deciphering insurance plans to making appointments and managing prescriptions. You're not alone in facing these uncertainties, and this chapter is here to demystify healthcare, empower you with knowledge, and help you make informed decisions about your well-being. So, let's dive in and unravel the intricacies of healthcare, ensuring that you're well-prepared to take charge of your health and make the best choices for your future. To begin our exploration of this chapter, let's start by clarifying some important terminology. This will provide you with a solid foundation and make it easier to grasp the concepts discussed in the upcoming sections.

Healthcare Terminology Explained

Premium: This is the regular payment you make to your health insurance company. Many individuals receive insurance coverage through their employers, with the premium automatically deducted from their paychecks. Alternatively, some individuals choose to purchase insurance independently, paying for it directly rather than going through their employer.

Deductible: The initial amount you must pay out of your pocket for covered healthcare services before your insurance starts covering costs. This does not mean you pay the full cost but instead you pay the contractual rate that the physician, practice or hospital has agreed to with the insurance company.

Co-pay (Co-payment): A fixed amount you pay for a specific healthcare service or prescription, often due at the time of service.

Co-insurance: The percentage of healthcare costs you share with your insurance company after you've met your deductible. Typically this is 80/20 or 90/10. Again, this is based on the contractual rate the physician, practice or hospital has agreed to with the insurance company.

Out-of-Pocket Maximum (OOPM): You must pay for covered services in a plan year, including deductibles, co-pays, and co-insurance. Once you reach this limit, your insurance covers all additional costs.

In-Network: Healthcare providers and facilities that have a contract with your insurance company to provide services at pre-negotiated rates. Visiting in-network providers typically costs less.

Out-of-Network: Healthcare providers and facilities that do not have a contract with your insurance company. Visiting out-of-network providers often results in higher costs for you.

Preventive Care: Services such as vaccinations and screenings that aim to prevent health issues before they occur. Many insurance plans cover preventive care at no cost to the insured.

Emergency Care: Immediate medical treatment for severe or life-threatening conditions, often covered by insurance even if the provider is out-of-network. This is typically only seen at hospitals such as the ER.

Primary Care Physician (PCP): is like your healthcare quarterback, a central figure in your medical journey. They offer general medical care, serve as your first point of contact for health issues, and play a vital role in preventive care.Many health insurance plans also require you to have a designated PCP to streamline your healthcare management.

Specialist: A doctor with expertise in a specific area of medicine, such as a cardiologist, dermatologist, or orthopedist.

Prescription Drug Coverage: Insurance coverage for medications may involve co-pays or co-insurance for each prescription.

Health Savings Account (HSA): A tax-advantaged savings account paired with a high-deductible health plan used to save money for medical expenses.

Flexible Spending Account (FSA): A pre-tax savings account for medical expenses, often offered through your employer.

Explanation of Benefits (EOB): A document from your insurance company that explains how a claim was processed, including what they paid and what you owe.

Open Enrollment: A specific period during which you can sign up for or change your health insurance plan, usually once a year.

Dependent Coverage: The option to include family members, such as children or spouses, under your health insurance policy.

Authorization: Approval from your insurer or provider before specific medical services, which is vital to ensure your insurance covers the service and prevents unexpected expenses.

Referral: A recommendation from your primary care physician to see a specialist for a specific medical issue, ensuring you get appropriate care from an expert in that area.

In simple terms, processing claims in healthcare works like this:

- You receive medical care.
- The healthcare provider sends a bill to your insurance company, detailing the services provided.
- Your insurance company reviews the bill and determines what expenses they'll cover based on your policy.
- You may need to pay any costs not covered by your insurance, known as "out-of-pocket expenses."
- You will receive a bill from the provider to let you know how much you owe
- You will receive a copy of the explanation of benefits from your insurance so be sure to match up your EOB with the bill from the provider to ensure there are no discrepancies

Healthcare Insurance

Understanding health insurance policies requires careful consideration of their costs, coverage, and healthcare provider selection process. Each plan offers a different balance of these elements, and choosing the right one depends heavily on your individual or family needs. It's crucial to review each policy thoroughly to determine which aligns best with your specific circumstances, even if you're still on your parents' coverage due to your age, you should understand the coverage to ensure you take appropriate steps to stay within the plan coverage.

When evaluating health plans, consider how frequently you or your family need medical care. If you have ongoing medical conditions or expect regular doctor visits, a plan with lower co-pays and a broad network of providers might be more beneficial despite potentially higher premiums. On the other hand, if you're generally healthy and seldom visit the doctor, a plan with lower monthly premiums but higher out-of-pocket costs for occasional care could be a more cost-effective choice.

Consider the immediate cost of premiums and how much you'd potentially pay out-of-pocket for services like specialist visits, prescriptions, and emergency care. Some plans may offer lower premiums but have higher deductibles and co-pays, which could cost more if you require frequent medical attention.

Additionally, think about the network of providers each plan offers. If you have preferred doctors or specialists, ensure they are included in the plan's network. If not, you might have to pay more to see out-of-network providers or choose a different plan altogether.

Lastly, consider any specific health needs you or your family may have. For example, if someone requires regular specialist care, mental health services, or maternity care, ensure the plan covers these adequately.

In summary, selecting the right health insurance policy balances cost, coverage, and convenience. It's vital to assess your personal and family health needs carefully and compare them against what each plan offers to make an informed decision that provides the best possible coverage for your situation.

Six Most Common Insurance Plans

HMOs (Health Maintenance Organizations):

- Limit coverage to network providers except in emergencies.
- Require primary care physician (PCP) referrals.
- Offer lower monthly rates and typically lower cost-sharing (deductibles, co-pays, out-of-pocket maximums) compared to PPOs, especially in employer-provided plans.
- Individual HMO plans may have out-of-pocket costs comparable to PPOs.

PPOs (Preferred Provider Organizations):

- Provide a preferred provider network but also cover out-of-network care.
- Feature higher monthly premiums and cost-sharing due to less restrictive networks.
- Have seen a decline in popularity as networks shrink and shift to EPOs and HMOs.
- Predominant in employer-sponsored plans but less common in individual markets, with some states no longer offering them.

EPOs (Exclusive Provider Organizations):

- Operate with a specific provider network and don't cover out-of-network care except in emergencies.
- Do not typically require a PCP referral for specialists.
- Function like PPOs but without out-of-network coverage.

POS (Point of Service) Plans:

- Blend features of HMOs and PPOs.
- Allow some out-of-network care under certain conditions.
- Often require PCP referrals for all medical services.

Indemnity Plans:

- Offer traditional fee-for-service coverage without managed care.
- Reimburse a percentage of charges for covered medical procedures.
- Have become rare in modern healthcare, with less than 1% of American workers with employer-sponsored health coverage using them.
- Most current medical policies offer managed care, though dental indemnity plans are still common.

HSA (Health Savings Accounts):

- It is not a specific type of managed care but can be used with various plans like HMOs, PPOs, EPOs, and POS.
- Must adhere to IRS guidelines on plan design.

The Significance of Health Insurance and What It Encompasses

In simple terms, health insurance is your financial safety net in the unpredictable world of healthcare. It's like having a friend who's got your back when you least expect it. So, why is it such a big deal, especially for a young adult like you? Let's break it down.

Financial Safety Net: Think of health insurance as your superhero cape for medical expenses. It's a legal agreement between you and an insurance company that steps in to cover the costs when you're hit with unexpected medical bills. Whether it's an illness, an accident, or any other covered event, health insurance ensures you're not drowning in medical debt.

Insurance Processing Methods: When it comes to paying your medical bills, your health insurance company does it in two ways:

- **In-Network Care:** If you seek treatment at a hospital or with doctors within your insurance network, you usually don't have to dig into your pockets during service. Your health plan takes care of the bills directly.

- **Out-of-Pocket Costs:** If you receive care outside of your network, you might need to pay some costs upfront, but you can later request reimbursement from your insurance provider.

Why It Matters – The Consequences of Going Without Health Insurance

While having health insurance offers a safety net, it's equally important to understand the potential downsides of not having coverage. Here's a glimpse into what could happen if you decide to go without health insurance:

Financial Ruin: Medical bills can skyrocket in the blink of an eye. Without insurance, you could find yourself drowning in debt, potentially leading to bankruptcy. Even routine check-ups and minor accidents can accumulate hefty bills, leaving you with a crippling financial burden.

Limited Access to Healthcare: Without insurance, your choices of healthcare providers and facilities may be restricted. You might hesitate to seek medical attention when needed, which could lead to delayed treatment and worsened health conditions.

Emergency Expenses: Imagine facing a sudden medical emergency, such as an accident or a severe illness. Without insurance, you'd be solely responsible for all the associated costs, including hospitalization, surgeries, and medication.

This can deplete your savings or force you to take on loans with high interest rates or worse, file bankruptcy.

Avoidance of Preventive Care: Routine check-ups and preventive measures are crucial for maintaining good health. Without insurance, you may skip these essential visits due to the fear of expenses. Missing out on preventive care can lead to undiagnosed health issues that could have been addressed early.

Stress and Anxiety: Constant worry about the financial implications of healthcare can take a toll on your mental health. The stress and anxiety of not having a safety net can negatively impact your overall well-being.

No Family Protection: If you have a family, going without health insurance jeopardizes your health and the well-being of your loved ones. An unexpected medical crisis could have a devastating ripple effect on your family's financial stability.

Legal Mandates: Depending on your location, there may be legal requirements to have health insurance. Going without it could result in penalties or fines, adding to your financial burden.

In essence, the absence of health insurance leaves you vulnerable to financial hardship, limited healthcare options, and unnecessary stress. It's not just about the cost of medical care; it's also about your peace of mind and the well-being of you and your family. Health insurance is a vital safety net to protect against the life-threatening consequences of being uninsured.

Choosing Providers and Booking Appointments with Confidence

We'll help you choose a primary care physician and grasp the essentials of scheduling appointments, ensuring you have the knowledge to navigate the healthcare system with confidence.

The objective is to discover a PCP who aligns with your criteria as outlined below.

Check In-Network Providers: Ensure your PCP is in your insurance network to save on costs.

Location Matters: Pick a PCP whose office is easy to reach from your college or home.

Read Reviews: Research PCPs online for feedback on their responsiveness and how they treat patients.

Flexible Hours: Look for a PCP with flexible hours to fit your college schedule.

Telehealth Options: Consider telehealth appointments for convenience and accessibility.

Scheduling: Book appointments online or by phone for your convenience.

Knowing When to Seek Care

Primary Care Physician (PCP):

- Routine check-ups and preventive care.
- Non-life-threatening illnesses or conditions.
- Managing chronic conditions.
- Prescription refills.
- Minor injuries or sprains.
- Follow-up on ongoing health issues.
- Non-severe cold or flu symptoms.
- General health concerns or questions.

Urgent Care:

- Minor injuries like cuts, burns, or minor fractures.
- Mild to moderate allergic reactions.
- Fever without severe symptoms.
- Sprains and strains.
- Minor infections (e.g., ear or sinus infections).
- Urinary tract infections (UTIs).
- Minor asthma or respiratory issues.
- Needed X-rays or lab tests after hours.
- Other non-life-threatening but urgent medical needs.

Emergency Room (ER):

- Severe injuries, such as head injuries, broken bones, or deep cuts.

- Chest pain or severe heart palpitations.
- Difficulty breathing or shortness of breath.
- Seizures or loss of consciousness.
- Severe allergic reactions (e.g., difficulty breathing, swelling of the face).
- Signs of a stroke (e.g., sudden weakness, confusion, trouble speaking).
- Severe abdominal pain.
- High fever with severe symptoms.
- Severe burns or electrical injuries.
- Severe bleeding or injuries after an accident.
- Suicidal thoughts or severe mental health crisis.

Considerations for College Students

Schedule-Friendly: Find healthcare providers who accommodate your busy college life.

Understand Costs: Know your insurance costs, deductibles, and co-payments. Save money by using in-network options.

Digital Accessibility: Explore providers with online appointment booking, telehealth, and medical record access.

Emergency Preparedness: Research nearby hospitals and urgent care centers and keep important medical records handy in emergencies.

So, there you have it—some essential insights to help you navigate the world of healthcare as a young adult. Remember, your health is an investment, and making informed decisions today will pay off in the long run. Don't hesitate to ask questions, explore your options, and stay proactive about your well-being.

Wellness Checks and Preventive Care: Your Health, Your Choice

Taking charge of your health is paramount, especially during the crucial phase of young adulthood. This section will delve into the significance of routine check-ups and preventive care, emphasizing their role in maintaining your well-being. Additionally, we'll provide insights into vaccinations, offering valuable information to empower your healthcare decisions.

The Value of Routine Check-ups

Emphasis on Prevention: Routine check-ups are not just for when you're feeling unwell. They serve as proactive health assessments to identify potential issues before they become major concerns. This approach not only keeps you healthier but can also reduce future healthcare costs.

Integrated Evaluation: Regular check-ups encompass your mental and emotional well-being beyond physical health. This holistic evaluation is particularly important as young adults face the changes and stresses of college or independent living.

Services for Prevention (Screenings, Vaccines, etc.)

A Review of Vaccines: Vaccinations are crucial in preventing various diseases. Staying informed about recommended vaccines is essential for your overall health. College-aged or not, vaccines protect you and the community.

Assessing Potential: Early screenings, such as those for STIs, high blood pressure, and cholesterol, are like health checkpoints. These screenings are tailored to your age and risk factors, identifying and addressing potential health problems promptly.

Primary Care Physician's Recommended Visit Frequency:

Notes on Particulars: Depending on your unique health situation, lifestyle, or mental health needs, you may require more frequent check-ups. Collaborate with your PCP to establish a suitable visit plan that aligns with your health goals.

Things to Bring to Your Doctor's Appointments and What to Ask

Addressing Health Issues: Open communication between you and your healthcare professional is key to understanding your condition fully. Preparing questions and providing detailed, honest information about your symptoms and lifestyle empowers your healthcare provider to make the best decisions for your health.

Making Sense of Treatment Programs: Treatment plans are more effective when you clearly understand them. Ask your healthcare provider about the reasoning behind treatment suggestions, potential side effects, and how to integrate these recommendations into your daily life, whether you're a college student or living independently.

Check for Mental Health: Your mental health directly impacts your physical well-being. Regardless of your age or living situation, be open and honest about any stress, difficulties, or mental health issues you're facing. Your PCP can provide support, referrals, or services if needed.

Vaccinations and Immunizations

Comprehending the Timetable for Vaccines: Staying updated on recommended vaccines, including booster shots if necessary, ensures the best protection against preventable diseases. Your vaccination needs can evolve as you transition from adolescence to adulthood.

Vaccinations Tailored to Your Needs: Some vaccines, like those for meningitis, are particularly important for young adults, especially if you're in college or living in shared housing. Discuss with your doctor before such transitions.

Common Vaccines for Young Adults: Besides standard vaccinations, young adults should consider getting the annual flu shot to protect themselves and those around them. The HPV vaccine is vital for cancer prevention, and vaccines like meningitis and Tdap are essential for maintaining good health.

Vaccination Locations

Healthcare on Campus: Many colleges offer vaccination services on campus, making it convenient for students. Check with your college's health services for information on available vaccines.

Primary Care Physician (PCP): Your PCP can offer tailored recommendations and administer them in the office, taking into account your medical history and current health condition.

Pharmacy and Health Centers: Vaccines are available at many local clinics and pharmacies. If you're a young adult living independently, inquire about vaccination services at your neighborhood pharmacy or health center.

Managing Prescriptions and Medications

Taking control of your health means understanding how to manage prescriptions and medications effectively. This knowledge is valuable for individuals of all ages. It's essential to be informed about your medications, their potential effects on your health, and how to use them responsibly. This proactive approach empowers you to make sound decisions and take charge of your well-being. Whether you have a chronic condition or require occasional treatments, responsible medication management is a crucial aspect of maintaining good health.

Understanding Your Medication

Purpose and Dosage: Knowing why you're taking a particular medication and the correct dosage is essential. Ask your healthcare provider about its function and the recommended dose.

Potential Side Effects: Don't hesitate to consult with your pharmacist about your medications, including potential side effects and what to do if they occur.

Managing Medication Dispensing

Choosing a Pharmacy: Convenience matters when it comes to refilling your prescriptions. Select a pharmacy with convenient hours and, if available, prescription delivery services.

Insurance Information: To minimize out-of-pocket costs, provide your insurance details when filling prescriptions. Familiarize yourself with co-payments and any additional expenses.

Utilizing Copay Cards: Ask your provider about copay cards that can help to reduce the cost of your prescription

GoodRx: GoodRx is a handy app and website that helps you find the best prices for your prescription medications. It provides a list of nearby pharmacies, along with the prices they charge, and offers access to discounts and coupons that can significantly lower your out-of-pocket costs. Whether you have insurance or not, GoodRx can be a valuable tool in reducing the financial burden of healthcare expenses."

Considering Generic Options: Generic medications are often more affordable and equally effective as brand-name ones. Discuss generic alternatives with your healthcare provider or pharmacist.

Tracking Prescription Refills: Don't forget when your prescriptions need refilling. Setting up automatic refills or using reminders can help you stay on track.

Ensuring Proper Medication Adherence

Follow Prescribed Instructions: The key to successful medication outcomes lies in strict adherence to your prescribed regimen. Always follow your healthcare provider's instructions regarding timing and dosage meticulously. If you ever have any uncertainties, don't hesitate to seek guidance from your healthcare professional. For instance, if you're prescribed a 10-day course of antibiotics, completing the full duration is crucial to effectively treating the underlying condition.

Safe Storage: Proper storage is crucial for maintaining medication effectiveness and safety. Always check the expiration date and store medications as directed (e.g., in a cool, dry place). Ensure the safety of your medications, especially when there are pets or young children in your environment, as their accidental access can lead to severe consequences.

Inform Your Healthcare Providers: Keeping your healthcare providers informed about changes in your health, new symptoms, or medication changes is essential for effective treatment. Immediately notify your doctor of any changes.

Addressing Potential Interactions: It's essential to grasp the potential for drug interactions to prevent any undesirable consequences. Have an open conversation with your healthcare provider or pharmacist about any worries regarding drug interactions. You can also utilize reliable websites like Drugs.com to evaluate potential drug interactions and make informed decisions about your medications.

Be Prepared: Unforeseen circumstances can occur, such as missed doses or adverse reactions. Create a plan for dealing with such situations or seek medical help when in doubt.

Understanding prescription drugs, the prescription-filling process, and medication safety procedures is essential for young adults, whether they're in college or not. Active participation in medication management ensures effective treatment and proactive health maintenance.

Estimates and Payment Options

Whether you're planning for dental, vision, or medical procedures, it's crucial to have a clear understanding of the associated costs. Taking this proactive approach helps you prepare financially and make well-informed decisions about your healthcare. It prevents unexpected bills, allows you to explore suitable payment plans, and ensures you maximize your insurance benefits. By taking these steps in advance, you can reduce stress and confidently manage the financial aspects of your healthcare.

Request Estimates: Ask your healthcare provider for a detailed estimate of the proposed treatment, including all associated costs.

Payment Plans: Many healthcare facilities offer flexible payment options, allowing you to spread the cost of treatment over several months.

Financing: Inquire about financing options to help cover the expenses of procedures, especially for more costly treatments.

Charity Care and Federal Poverty Discounts: Additionally, some healthcare institutions offer charity care programs and federal poverty discounts for individuals or families who meet specific income criteria. These programs can provide significant financial relief, so don't hesitate to inquire about them if needed.

Understanding your insurance coverage, exploring coverage options, reviewing benefits for various procedures, and obtaining estimates for healthcare services while considering payment plans and financing can empower you to make informed decisions about your health and effectively manage the financial aspects of your care.

Dental Health and Oral Care

As you step into adulthood, prioritizing your oral health becomes paramount. It goes beyond having a captivating smile; it profoundly influences your overall well-being. In this section, we will embark on a journey to explore the vital facets of dental health and oral care, equipping you with the wisdom and practices necessary for a lifetime filled with healthy smiles and optimal health. Remember those lessons from childhood about regular teeth brushing, flossing, and those routine dentist visits? Now, let's uncover why these practices are indispensable for your oral health as you navigate the path to adulthood.

The Value of Good Oral Hygiene

Preventive Characteristics: Maintaining good oral health is your first defense against issues like cavities and gum disease. Regular oral care practices are key to preserving the health and longevity of your teeth and gums.

The Importance of Oral Health to Total Health: Oral health is intricately connected to your overall well-being. Neglecting oral hygiene can have far-reaching consequences, potentially contributing to broader health problems. A healthy mouth is a cornerstone of good health in general.

Locating a Dentist and Making Appointments for Dental Treatment

Access to Dental Services: Ensuring easy access to dental care is essential. Whether in an urban or rural area, finding a local dentist and establishing a consistent dental care routine guarantees that your oral health needs are met.

Making Regular Appointments: Consistency is key when it comes to oral health. Regular dental check-ups are preventive measures that help detect and address oral health issues early, allowing for timely intervention and treatment. Most insurances cover a dental cleaning 2x per year.

Dental Plans and Their Coverage

Dental insurance and coverage options are essential considerations when it comes to managing the costs of dental care. Here's what you need to know:

Dental Insurance: Dental insurance can provide financial assistance for routine and emergency dental care. To make the most of your coverage, familiarize yourself with your policy, including:

- **Covered Services:** Know which dental services are covered by your insurance, such as preventive care, basic procedures, and major treatments.

- **Benefits Breakdown:** Pay attention to the details of your benefits, especially for common procedures like cavity repair, root canals, braces, and more. Understand what percentage of the cost is covered by your insurance.

Coverage Options: In addition to individual dental insurance plans, consider other options:

- **Health Plans:** Some health insurance plans include dental coverage as an add-on or part of a comprehensive package.
- **Employer-Sponsored Plans:** If employed, your employer may offer dental insurance as part of your benefits package.
- **Supplemental Dental Plans:** These plans can complement your existing coverage or fill gaps in dental care.

Helpful Hints for Keeping Your Teeth Clean

Effective Oral Hygiene Practices: Consistently brushing and flossing teeth is the cornerstone of good oral hygiene. These simple habits prevent plaque buildup, support healthy gums, and reduce the risk of cavities. For best results, brush 2x per day, and floss at least once per day.

Mindful Diet Choices: Be conscious of your diet, particularly sugary foods and beverages. Reducing sugar intake can significantly lower the risk of tooth decay and oral health problems.

Emphasizing Fluoride: Fluoride is essential for strengthening tooth enamel and preventing cavities. Incorporate fluoride toothpaste into your daily oral care routine and consider fluoride treatments if your dentist recommends.

Oral Safety During Physical Activities: Protecting your teeth during sports and physical activities is crucial. Wearing a mouthguard can prevent dental injuries, preserving your oral health.

Avoiding Harmful Habits: Limiting alcohol consumption and abstaining from smoking are essential for oral health. These habits can worsen oral health problems and negatively impact your overall well-being.

Your oral health is a vital component of your overall health. By understanding the importance of dental health, finding a local dentist, navigating dental insurance, and practicing effective oral hygiene, you'll be well-equipped to ensure a lifetime of healthy smiles and optimal well-being.

Clear Vision: Nurturing Your Eye Health

Clear vision is a window to the world and a vital component of your overall well-being, especially as a young adult. In this section, we'll delve into the importance of eye care, focusing on annual eye exams and vision-related considerations that can impact your academic and personal life. Let's explore how prioritizing your eye health can pave the way for a future filled with clear vision and optimal performance.

Why It's Crucial to Have Annual Eye Exams

Preventive: Regular eye exams play a crucial role in preventive care, helping to identify potential issues before they escalate into major concerns. Make it a priority to schedule these check-ups to keep a close watch on your eye health. Typical exams are done at least annually.

Academic & Career Impact: Maintaining optimal vision is not merely a matter of eye health; it profoundly influences academic excellence and professional accomplishments. Impaired eyesight can hinder your academic performance by affecting your reading, writing, and learning ability. Moreover, in the professional sphere, vision problems may undermine your career by impeding your performance, limiting job opportunities, and affecting your overall success. Whether you're a student striving for academic excellence or a professional aiming to advance in your career, the importance of clear vision cannot be underestimated.

Safe Driving: Annual vision exams are essential for maintaining good eyesight and play a crucial role in safe driving. These regular check-ups help detect changes in your vision that could affect your ability to drive safely, such as refractive errors or eye conditions. By addressing vision issues promptly through annual exams, you can ensure that you have a clear and accurate vision on the road, contributing to safer driving experiences for yourself and others.

Seeking the Services of an Eye Doctor

Local Eye Care Professionals: Building a relationship with a nearby optometrist or ophthalmologist guarantees ongoing and accessible eye care. Young adults, inquire about vision care options in your neighborhood. When in doubt, seek recommendations from others.

Why You Should Get Your Eyes Examined Regularly

Optimal Vision and Early Detection: Regular eye exams offer two invaluable benefits – maintaining optimal vision and detecting potential problems early. Follow your eye doctor's advice and schedule regular check-ups every year or as recommended.

Understanding Vision Insurance and Maximizing Benefits

Navigating vision insurance is crucial to effectively manage the costs of eye care. Here are some valuable tips to consider:

Vision Insurance Overview: Vision insurance typically covers some of the costs associated with eye care, including eye exams, eyeglasses, and contact lenses. However, the specifics of coverage can vary from one plan to another.

Know Your Plan: Review your vision insurance policy carefully. Pay attention to:

- **Coverage Limits:** Some vision insurance plans restrict how often they cover certain services. For example, they may only provide coverage for a new pair of eyeglasses or contact lenses every other year.

- **Dollar Amounts:** Many plans have a maximum amount they'll pay for eyeglasses or contact lenses. Anything beyond this limit becomes your responsibility.
- **In-Network Providers:** Find out which eye doctors and optical centers are in-network. Visiting in-network providers often results in lower out-of-pocket expenses.
- **Estimate Costs:** Before committing to vision care services, request your eye care provider's estimates. This can help you understand the potential out-of-pocket expenses and make informed decisions.
- **Compare Options:** If your insurance plan covers eyeglasses and contact lenses, compare the costs and benefits of each option. Some plans may provide more generous coverage for one type of corrective eyewear.
- **Utilize Flexible Spending Accounts (FSAs) or Health Savings Accounts (HSAs):** If you have an FSA or HSA, consider using these tax-advantaged accounts to pay for vision-related expenses not covered by insurance.

Prescription Updates: If your prescription changes, update your eyeglasses or contact lenses accordingly. Wearing the correct prescription helps maintain clear vision and prevents eye strain.

Inquire About Discounts: Some vision insurance plans offer discounts on additional services, such as laser eye surgery or designer eyewear frames. Don't hesitate to ask your provider about available discounts.

By knowing the specifics of your vision insurance plan, estimating costs before committing to eye care services, and maximizing your benefits, you can effectively manage your eye health while optimizing your insurance coverage.

Mastering Eyewear Choices and Responsible Usage

Eyeglass Frames: When selecting eyeglass frames, consider factors like comfort, style, and how they complement your face shape and lifestyle. As a young adult, your frames should reflect your style and cater to your active life.

Proper Care of Contact Lenses: Maintaining clean and infection-free contact lenses is essential for preserving good vision. Always use the prescribed cleaning solution and practice thorough handwashing before handling lenses.

Using eyewear Responsibly: Responsible eyewear use is vital. Avoid leaving contacts in for extended periods, as it can lead to issues like ulcers. Use your glasses when required and follow your eye doctor's recommendations.

Preventing Eye Strain: Extended screen time can lead to eye strain. Remember the 20-20-20 rule – take a 20-second break every 20 minutes and focus on something 20 feet away to alleviate eye strain caused by screen use.

Prioritizing your eye health through regular exams, finding a local eye care professional, understanding vision insurance, practicing proper eyeglasses and contact lens care, and using your eyewear responsibly are essential steps to ensure clear vision and peak performance in your academic and personal pursuits.

Key Takeaways

Understanding Health Insurance

- When choosing health insurance, carefully evaluate costs, coverage, and provider networks based on your healthcare needs.
- Consider potential out-of-pocket expenses, including deductibles and co-pays.
- Ensure your preferred healthcare providers are in-network, and assess coverage for specific health needs.

The Significance of Health Insurance

- Health insurance serves as a financial safety net, covering unexpected medical expenses.
- Going without health insurance can lead to financial ruin, limited healthcare access, and avoidance of preventive care.
- It provides peace of mind and safeguards your family's financial stability.

Wellness Checks and Preventive Care

- Routine check-ups are essential for proactive health assessments.
- Early screenings, vaccinations, and regular visits to a primary care physician help maintain good health.
- Effective communication with healthcare providers is crucial for understanding your health condition and treatment plans.

Clear Vision and Eye Health

- Annual eye exams are vital for maintaining optimal vision and preventing vision-related issues.
- Good eye health positively impacts academic and career success and safe driving.
- Understand your vision insurance coverage, seek services from local eye care professionals, and make responsible eyewear choices.

Test Your Knowledge

1. Why is it important to have health insurance if you can?

- a. To avoid taxes
- b. To get discounts on gym memberships
- c. To protect yourself from high medical costs
- d. To receive free healthcare

2. Why are wellness visits and preventive care important?

- a. They help you avoid going to the gym
- b. They ensure you get sick often
- c. They detect and prevent health issues early
- d. They provide opportunities to eat more junk food

3. How can getting an estimate of cost help you?

- a. It enables you to win a bet with your friends
- b. It allows you to plan your budget and make informed decisions
- c. It enables you to avoid medical appointments altogether
- d. It guarantees you the lowest price for any medical service

4. How can you help keep your oral care healthy?

- a. By brushing and flossing regularly and scheduling dental check-ups.
- b. By eating a balanced diet and limiting sugary snacks.
- c. By avoiding tobacco and excessive alcohol consumption.
- d. All of the above.

5. What is the difference between in and out-of-network?

- a. In-network providers offer better and cheaper services
- b. In-network is for weekdays, out-of-network is for weekends
- c. In-network providers have agreements with your insurance company, while out-of-network providers do not
- d. In-network providers are located indoors, while out-of-network providers are located outdoors

6. A fixed amount you pay for a service is called what?

- a. Co-insurance
- b. Out-of-pocket
- c. Premium
- d. Co-pay

2 RELATIONSHIPS AND SEXUAL HEALTH

Let me introduce you to Alex – a young adult who found themselves in a bit of a pickle because they didn't have the right info about relationships and sexual health.

So, picture this: Alex started seeing someone they really liked, and things got pretty serious. They wanted to take their relationship to the next level but didn't know how to have an open and honest conversation about it. They felt kinda awkward bringing up the topic of consent and protection because, well, they'd never really talked about it with anyone.

Long story short, Alex and their partner ended up in a situation where lines got blurred, and they didn't discuss their boundaries or use protection. Unfortunately, this resulted in Alex contracting a sexually transmitted infection (STI). It was a bit of a mess, and it left Alex feeling confused and worried about their health.

Alex had to take the responsible step of seeking medical treatment. They made an appointment with a healthcare provider, and during that visit, they had to have an open and honest conversation about what had happened. It was a bit uncomfortable, but it was crucial for their health and well-being.

Now, Alex faces the challenge of discussing this information with any potential new partners in the future, emphasizing the importance of clear communication, consent, and protection in intimate relationships.

Now, here's the kicker – all this could have been avoided with some knowledge about consent, protection, and open communication. That's exactly what this chapter is here for – to make sure you don't have to learn things the hard way like Alex did. We're going to equip you with the tools and know-how to handle these situations confidently and responsibly. So, let's dive in and make sure you're prepared for whatever comes your way!

How to Be Safe on Dates

Ensuring Your Safety During Dates

Dating can be an exciting and enjoyable experience, but it's essential to prioritize safety for everyone, regardless of gender. Whether meeting someone for the first time or going on subsequent dates, taking precautionary measures ensures a secure and enjoyable dating experience. Here are key strategies on how to stay safe during your dates:

Personal Safety Precautions

Trust Your Instincts: Always listen to your gut feelings. If something feels off or uncomfortable during a date, prioritize your safety. Trusting your intuition can help you make quick decisions to protect yourself.

Limit Personal Information: As you're getting to know someone, it's important to strike a balance between sharing and safeguarding your personal information. It's a good idea to hold back on sharing things like your home address, financial details, or sensitive personal history in the early stages of the relationship. Instead, focus on building trust and gradually sharing these aspects of your life as your relationship deepens and you feel more comfortable doing so.

Be Mindful of Alcohol Consumption: If you consume alcohol during your date, do so responsibly. Watch your drink at all times; never leave it unattended. Know your limits and avoid excessive drinking. Being in control of your faculties is crucial for personal safety.

Communicating Your Plans

Inform Someone You Trust:

1. Before going on a date, inform a trusted friend or family member about your plans.

2. Share details such as the location, time, and who you'll be meeting.

3. Provide periodic updates if plans change or if you decide to go to a different location.

Establish a Check-In System: Set up a check-in system with a friend during the date. This could involve sending a quick text at a predetermined time to confirm that you're okay. If your date extends into the evening, periodic check-ins can provide peace of mind.

Emergency Code Word: Create a word or phrase with a friend. If you feel uncomfortable or need assistance during the date, you can discreetly use this code to signal that you need help. This code can be useful for communicating distress without alarming your date.

Meeting in Public Places

Choose Public Venues: Opt for public places for the first few dates. Coffee shops, restaurants, or public parks provide a safer environment with other people around. Public venues also offer an easy exit if you need to leave the date quickly.

Daytime Meetings: Consider daytime meetings for initial encounters. Daylight hours generally offer increased visibility and a more secure atmosphere. It's easier to assess your date's character in well-lit settings.

Avoid Private Residences Initially: Refrain from visiting private residences or inviting someone to your home during the early stages of dating. Getting to know each other in public settings is safer, where you can gauge compatibility without compromising your safety.

Sharing Location Details

Share Live Location: Use location-sharing features on your smartphone with a trusted friend. Many messaging apps offer this option, allowing someone to track your live location during the date. Sharing your location can be reassuring for both you and your loved ones.

Emergency Services App: Consider using safety apps designed for emergencies. These apps often include features like panic buttons and location tracking. Quick access to emergency services or designated contacts can provide an extra layer of security.

Stay Connected: Keep your phone charged and stay connected throughout the date. Ensure you have a means of communication in case you need assistance or need to make an emergency call. A charged phone can be a lifeline in unexpected situations.

Dating should be an enjoyable and positive experience; these safety precautions are intended to help ensure it remains so. By prioritizing personal safety, communicating your plans, meeting in public places, and sharing location details, you contribute to a safer dating environment for yourself and others.

Online Dating Safety Tips for Young Adults

Online dating has become a common way for people to meet

and connect. While it provides exciting opportunities, prioritizing safety and informed choices is crucial. Here are essential tips to navigate online dating securely:

Creating a Secure Online Profile

Your online dating profile is your digital introduction, and creating a secure profile is the first step in establishing a positive online presence while safeguarding your privacy.

Here's how to do it:

Limit Personal Information: Avoid sharing sensitive details in your profile, such as home address, phone number, or financial information. These should be reserved for private conversations once trust has been established.

Unique Photos: Use unique and recent photos for your profile. Avoid using images that can be reverse-searched to find your identity. This helps protect your privacy and ensures authenticity.

Mindful Username: Choose a username that doesn't reveal too much personal information. Avoid using your full name or anything easily associated with your offline identity.

Privacy Settings: Familiarize yourself with the privacy settings of the dating platform. Adjust settings to control who can view your profile and contact you. This step allows you to manage your online visibility effectively.

Safety Precautions for Online Interactions

Engaging in online conversations requires safety precautions to create a secure and positive environment.

Messaging within the App: Keep initial communications within the dating app's messaging system. Avoid sharing personal contact information until you've established a level of trust. This adds a layer of security.

Beware of Red Flags: Be vigilant for red flags such as requests for money, overly aggressive behavior, or inconsistencies in the information provided. Report any suspicious activity to the platform administrators.

Avoid Clicking on Suspicious Links: Be cautious about clicking on links shared by someone you've just met online. These links could lead to phishing sites or malware. Verify the legitimacy of any links before clicking.

Report Inappropriate Behavior: Most dating platforms have reporting features. If you encounter inappropriate behavior or harassment, promptly report it to the platform administrators. This helps maintain a safe community.

Online Photo Safety: Online safety is paramount, so it's crucial to remember not to send photos of yourself, especially anything you wouldn't want others to see. Once an image is shared online, it can be challenging to control where it ends up, so always exercise caution and think twice before hitting that send button.

Meeting Online Contacts Offline

- When meeting online contacts offline, remember to prioritize safety and refer back to the 'How to Be Safe on Dates' section for valuable tips and precautions.

Cultivating Healthy and Fulfilling Romantic Relationships

Your transition into young adulthood opens up a world of opportunities, including exploring the intricacies of romantic relationships. Building these connections involves effective communication, self-awareness, conflict resolution skills, and setting clear boundaries and expectations. Here's a comprehensive guide to help you navigate the path of healthy romance:

Effective Communication in Relationships

Open and Honest Dialogue: Create an environment where you and your partner feel safe expressing your thoughts and feelings without judgment. Open communication is the foundation of a strong bond. To truly understand your partner's perspective, practice active listening. Take a moment to reflect on their words before responding – it's a powerful way to nurture mutual understanding.

Expressing Needs and Desires: Clear communication of your needs, desires, and expectations can prevent misunderstandings and lay the groundwork for trust within your relationship.

Non-Verbal Communication: Pay attention to non-verbal cues like body language, such as maintaining eye contact, and facial expressions like smiles and laughter; sometimes, they convey more than words ever could.

Respectful Disagreement: Disagreements are part of any relationship, but it's vital to handle them respectfully. Avoid personal attacks and focus on the issue at hand – this fosters a healthier conflict resolution process.

Recognizing Red Flags and Warning Signs

Lack of Respect: Watch for signs of disrespect, such as belittling comments or dismissive behavior. A healthy relationship thrives on mutual respect and appreciation. It's important to value and uplift each other, recognizing the worth and feelings of both partners.

Controlling Behavior: Be cautious of controlling tendencies. Healthy relationships are based on autonomy and mutual decision-making rather than one person exerting dominance. Remember that both individuals should have equal say and influence in the relationship.

Isolation: It may raise concerns if your partner isolates you from friends and family. Healthy relationships encourage social connections and personal growth. Being supportive of each other's social lives and personal development is a sign of a strong partnership.

Unwillingness to Compromise: Inflexibility and an unwillingness to compromise can indicate potential issues.

Successful relationships involve give-and-take to meet each other's needs. Flexibility and compromise are key ingredients for a harmonious relationship.

Consistent Dishonesty: Trust is the foundation of any healthy relationship, and consistent dishonesty can erode it. Be attentive to any signs of deception. Building trust through honesty and transparency is essential for a strong and lasting bond.

Conflict Resolution Strategies

Stay Calm: Emotions can run high during conflicts but strive to keep them in check. Communicating calmly helps prevent tensions from escalating. Maintaining a level head can lead to more productive discussions.

Focus on the Issue: Address the issue causing conflict rather than bringing up unrelated grievances. This approach maintains clarity and relevance, making it easier to find solutions to specific problems.

Seek Compromise: Aim for compromise. Finding a middle ground allows both partners to feel heard and respected. Compromise is a key aspect of healthy conflict resolution.

Take Breaks When Needed: If emotions become overwhelming, taking breaks can provide clarity and perspective before revisiting the discussion. Sometimes stepping away briefly can help you come back to the issue with a fresh perspective.

Learn from Conflicts: View conflicts as opportunities for growth. Understanding each other's perspectives and learning from disagreements strengthens the relationship. Conflict can be a catalyst for positive change and greater understanding.

By mastering these effective communication techniques, spotting potential warning signs, and using conflict resolution strategies, you'll find yourself navigating the intricate world of romantic relationships with confidence. Setting clear boundaries and expectations is key, helping you focus on healthy, respectful, and growth-oriented connections. It's all part of your journey towards meaningful and fulfilling relationships.

Understanding Sexual Health

Alright, folks, it's time to switch gears and dive into a topic that might make some of you blush, but hey, it's a part of growing up, right? We're talking about sexual health – a crucial aspect of your well-being as you navigate the maze of young adulthood. This chapter isn't about awkward lectures or shying away from the subject. It's about giving you the knowledge and tools to make informed choices and ensure a healthy, respectful, and enjoyable journey in this aspect of your life. So, brace yourselves for some important, honest, and open conversations as we explore the ins and outs of sexual health.

Responsible and Safe Sexual Practices

Engaging in responsible sexual practices is a fundamental aspect of maintaining the well-being of both partners.

Here are key considerations for a healthy and safe approach to intimacy:

Using Protection: Using protection, such as condoms and other contraception methods, plays a crucial role in keeping both partners safe from STIs and unplanned pregnancies. It's a shared responsibility that ensures the well-being of everyone involved.

Talking About Protection: Open and honest communication with your partner about contraception is essential. It's about making sure you're both on the same page when it comes to your sexual health. Discussing preferences and choices is a vital part of the conversation.

Getting Tested: Regular STI tests are a smart move, especially if you're in a non-monogamous relationship. These tests help catch any potential issues early, allowing for prompt treatment and preventing the spread of infections.

Knowing Each Other's Status: Honesty about your STI status and being informed about your partner's status is crucial. It's a way to build trust and maintain safe practices in your relationship, ensuring everyone's well-being.

Trying Other Things: Exploring non-penetrative sexual activities can be a fun and safe way to enjoy intimacy. Before trying anything new, have an open and respectful discussion with your partner to establish boundaries and preferences.

Taking Care of Your Reproductive Health: Regular check-ups with your healthcare provider cover various aspects of reproductive health. These check-ups address everything from contraception options to discussions about fertility.

Checking Your Contraception: If you're using hormonal contraception, remember to schedule regular check-ups to ensure it remains the right choice for you and is effective in meeting your needs.

Mental Well-being Matters: Your mental health is connected to your sexual well-being. During check-ups, don't hesitate to discuss any concerns related to your sexual experiences or relationships, as it's essential for your overall well-being.

Understanding Consent

Consent is a mutual and voluntary agreement among all parties involved in a sexual activity. It must be clear, enthusiastic, and can be changed or withdrawn at any time. So, always make sure all individuals involved are on the same page and comfortable with what's happening.

Key Points on Consent:

Communication is Key: Understanding consent requires open communication between sexual partners. Discussing boundaries, desires, and expectations before engaging in any sexual activity is fundamental for a consensual and respectful experience.

Freely Given: Consent must be given freely without coercion, manipulation, or pressure. It should never be assumed or obtained through force or intimidation. Everyone involved should feel entirely comfortable with the decisions being made.

Capacity to Consent: Individuals must possess the capacity to consent, meaning they are of legal age, mentally competent, and not under the influence of substances that impair judgment. Consent is not valid if any of the parties cannot give it.

Revocable: Consent can be revoked at any point during the sexual activity. The activity should cease immediately if someone expresses discomfort or changes their mind. Respecting boundaries is essential for a healthy experience.

As you embrace sexual health education, tap into the resources available to you, and make safe practices a part of your lives, you'll be well-equipped to confidently navigate the intricate world of intimate relationships. Your focus on well-being, respect for one another, and your journey of growth isn't just for your younger years – it's a foundation for a fulfilling future.

Key Takeaways

Prioritize Personal Safety in Dating: When dating, always prioritize personal safety. Trust your instincts, limit initial personal information sharing, and communicate your plans with someone you trust. Taking precautions ensures a secure and enjoyable dating experience.

Online Dating Safety: For those exploring online dating, create a secure online profile by limiting personal information, using unique photos, and familiarizing yourself with privacy settings. Practice safe online interactions and meet online contacts in public places initially.

Understand Sexual Health: Comprehensive sexual education is crucial for making informed decisions about sexual health, including contraception, consent, and responsible practices. It fosters respect and inclusivity and reduces the stigma surrounding sexual health topics.

Healthy Romantic Relationships: Cultivate healthy and fulfilling romantic relationships through effective communication, recognizing warning signs, employing conflict resolution strategies, and setting clear boundaries and expectations. Prioritize emotional safety, trust, and mutual growth.

Test Your Knowledge

1. What is an essential aspect of cultivating healthy romantic relationships?

- a. Avoiding communication
- b. Being secretive about your feelings
- c. Open and honest communication
- d. Ignoring each other's needs

2. Why is it crucial to practice safe dating on dates?

- a. To impress your date
- b. To maintain a sense of mystery
- c. To ensure your safety
- d. To make the date more exciting

3. What is an integral part of understanding sexual health?

- a. Practicing safe sex
- b. Regular health check-ups
- c. Being informed about contraceptives
- d. All of the above

4. Which of the following is an example of an unhealthy romantic relationship?

- a. Open communication and mutual respect
- b. Regular conflict resolution
- c. Emotional abuse and control
- d. Shared responsibilities

5. What does consent mean in the context of sexual activity?

- a. It means agreeing to engage in sexual activity without any prior communication.
- b. It implies that only verbal consent is required.
- c. It signifies the voluntary, clear, and enthusiastic agreement by all parties involved.

- d. It encompasses clear communication, mutual agreement, and willingness from all parties involved.

3 SOCIAL ETIQUETTE

In our fast-paced world, social interactions shape our daily lives. Think about the time you walked into your significant other's home to meet their parents for the first time, filled with excitement and nervousness, or the moments spent mingling at a family gathering, hoping to make a positive impression. Imagine engaging in online conversations, where words can have a lasting impact.

Now, let me share a story with you. Meet Brandon, a teenager getting ready to meet their partner's family for the first time. Brandon was eager to make a great impression, but he underestimated the importance of social etiquette. During dinner, Brandon started talking loudly about a topic that made some family members uncomfortable, and because Brandon was not watching for other's reactions or noticing that they were not engaging, this led to awkward silences and a less-than-pleasant atmosphere.

Now, imagine if Brandon had known the art of social etiquette. They would have been mindful of the conversation topics, listened actively to what others had to say, and used their manners at the dinner table. The interaction would have been smoother, and Brandon would have left a positive impression on their partner's family.

In various scenarios, understanding the nuances of social etiquette isn't just a skill; it's your secret weapon. It's the key that unlocks doors to success, be it in your personal relationships, social gatherings, or the digital realm.

This chapter on social etiquette is more than just a guide; it's your practical toolkit for navigating the world of social interactions. It offers tips and insights to help you present yourself confidently, treat others respectfully, and create meaningful connections in various social settings. With practical advice that's easy to follow and culturally sensitive, this chapter empowers you to navigate the social landscape with grace and courtesy, ensuring your interactions are not just pleasant but also profoundly impactful.

Introduction to Social Etiquette

In the complex world of social interactions, knowing your way around social etiquette is like having a superpower. It can make a huge difference in how people see you, the connections you make, and how your interactions play out. This chapter is your guide to mastering social etiquette, specifically tailored for teens and young adults. We'll dive into why it matters and how it can supercharge your social life.

Understanding the Significance of Social Etiquette

Social etiquette is the compass that guides us through the labyrinth of social interactions. It encompasses the unwritten rules that govern behavior, communication, and courtesy in various social settings. For young adults stepping into adulthood, grasping the importance of social etiquette is paramount. It transcends mere politeness; it manifests respect, consideration, and cultural awareness in our diverse and dynamic world.

By adhering to social etiquette, individuals signal their understanding of societal norms, radiating sophistication and awareness that leads to positive impressions. Recognizing the significance of social etiquette lays the foundation for successful interactions, whether in professional arenas, social gatherings, or personal relationships. It paves the way for meaningful connections and underscores an individual's commitment to gracefully navigating the intricate tapestry of social spaces.

How Proper Etiquette Enhances Your Social Interactions

Proper etiquette is the oil that lubricates the gears of social engagement, ensuring smoother and more positive interactions. It elevates the quality of relationships and contributes to a harmonious and respectful social environment. Here's how proper etiquette enhances our social interactions:

- **First Impressions:** As the saying goes, first impressions are lasting impressions. Exhibiting proper etiquette from the outset leaves a lasting, favorable mark on others. Whether in a job interview, meeting new acquaintances, or attending social functions, a well-mannered demeanor establishes a positive bedrock for future interactions.
- **Building Trust and Respect:** Etiquette is the cornerstone of trust and respect among individuals. Respectful behavior, active listening, and consideration for others' feelings create an atmosphere of trust. This is particularly pivotal in professional settings, where trust is integral to collaboration and success.
- **Cultural Sensitivity:** Social etiquette extends to cultural sensitivity. Recognizing and respecting cultural differences in greetings, gestures, and communication styles demonstrates global awareness and receptiveness to diverse perspectives. This, in turn, fosters inclusivity in social interactions.
- **Effective Communication:** Etiquette plays a pivotal role in effective communication. It guides individuals in expressing themselves respectfully, resolving conflicts diplomatically, and engaging in conversations without causing discomfort. Effective communication stands as the bedrock of successful social interactions.

- **Professional Advancement:** In the professional world, adherence to proper etiquette is a stepping stone to career advancement. Whether at networking events, business meetings, or workplace interactions, individuals with polished social skills are more likely to be considered for opportunities and promotions.
- **Positive Atmosphere in Social Spaces:** Proper etiquette contributes to a positive and comfortable atmosphere in social spaces. Whether attending formal events or casual gatherings, individuals who observe social norms create an environment where everyone feels valued and at ease.

Now that you're all set to boost your social skills, let's dive into various social situations and learn how to handle them with confidence and grace.

Mastering Group Social Events

Inviting Friends or Colleagues to Social Events

Effective Communication: When inviting friends or colleagues to social events, clear communication is key. Providing essential event details, such as the date, time, venue, and any special instructions, helps your guests plan their schedules and ensures everyone is on the same page. Make RSVPing easy, whether it's through a text message or a digital invitation that allows a simple click to RSVP.

Consideration for Preferences: Extend invitations thoughtfully by considering the preferences and availability of those you invite. Opt for event times and types that accommodate diverse interests and commitments. This approach increases the likelihood of a successful and enjoyable gathering.

Inclusive Invitations: Prioritize inclusivity when extending invitations. Avoid language or behaviors that might inadvertently make others feel excluded. Creating a welcoming and comfortable environment for all attendees enhances the overall experience.

RSVP Etiquette: When sending out invitations, it's a good practice to request RSVPs from your invitees. This not only helps with event planning but also ensures that everyone can anticipate and enjoy the gathering without any logistical surprises.

Choosing the Right Venue for Gatherings

Consider Group Size: Select venues based on the size of your group, ensuring that the chosen location can comfortably accommodate all attendees. Overcrowded spaces can hinder social interactions, so be mindful of the number of guests.

Variety of Venues: Diversify your venue choices based on the nature of the gathering. Opt for settings that align with the occasion, whether it's a casual coffee shop for a low-key meet-up, a vibrant restaurant for a birthday celebration, or a formal venue for a special event. Adapting the venue to the occasion enhances the overall experience.

Accessibility: Factor in the venue's accessibility, location, transportation options, and any special needs of your guests. Ensure that everyone can easily reach the location, taking into consideration factors like proximity to public transport and parking availability.

Ambiance and Atmosphere: Pay attention to the ambiance and atmosphere of the chosen venue. The setting should complement the mood of the event, such as a cozy cafe for a relaxed gathering or a more upscale restaurant for formal occasions. The right ambiance enhances the overall enjoyment of the gathering.

Dressing Appropriately for Different Occasions

Understand the Dress Code: Familiarize yourself with the event's dress code, whether it's casual, business casual, or formal attire. Dressing appropriately demonstrates respect for the occasion and consideration for fellow attendees, ensuring you blend seamlessly into the social setting.

Grooming and Personal Hygiene: Prioritize grooming and personal hygiene when preparing for social events. A well-groomed appearance leaves a positive impression and shows that you value your appearance in social settings.

Adapt to the Occasion: Adjust your attire to match the specific occasion, reflecting your understanding of the event's nature and showing respect for fellow attendees. Being in sync with the occasion helps you feel more comfortable and confident in your interactions.

Comfort and Confidence: Choose outfits that adhere to the dress code while also making you feel comfortable and confident. Your self-assured appearance positively influences your social interactions, allowing you to engage more effectively with others.

Being Punctual and Considerate of Others' Time

Value Others' Time: Demonstrating respect for others' schedules by valuing their time is crucial in social interactions. Punctuality underscores your consideration for their commitments and contributes to a pleasant social experience.

Plan Ahead: Organize your schedule to ensure you can arrive on time for social events. Take into account factors like traffic, transportation options, and any necessary preparations to avoid unnecessary delays.

Communication in Case of Delay: If you anticipate a delay, communicate promptly with the host or other attendees. Transparency about delays not only shows respect for others' time but also helps manage expectations and minimize inconvenience.

Avoiding Overstaying: In casual get-togethers, it's essential to be mindful of the gathering's duration. Be considerate of others' time commitments, and if you notice that the event is winding down, gracefully make your exit to avoid overstaying your welcome.

Handling Seating Arrangements and Table Manners in Various Settings

Observing Social Cues: Pay close attention to social cues regarding seating arrangements. In more formal settings, wait for guidance on where to sit, whereas in casual settings, choose an appropriate seat. Respect for social cues ensures a smoother start to the event.

Table Manners and Digital Etiquette: Adhering to good table manners is essential. Use utensils correctly, engage in polite conversation, and be mindful of your surroundings. Remember that excusing yourself to take a phone call or staying off devices from messaging and scrolling through apps is considered best practice, ensuring that you maintain a respectful and pleasant dining experience for everyone. Good table manners and digital etiquette contribute to a positive dining experience for all those sharing the meal with you.

Adapting to Cultural Norms: In multicultural settings, it's considerate to acquaint yourself with basic cultural norms related to seating arrangements and table manners. This respect for diverse practices fosters a harmonious social environment and ensures that you're sensitive to the preferences of others.

Consideration for Dietary Preferences: When organizing events, take into account the dietary preferences and restrictions of your attendees. Choose venues that offer diverse menu options to accommodate varying tastes.

Managing Contributions in Potluck Events

Potluck events involve contributions from multiple participants, and coordinating these contributions requires
thoughtful planning:

Coordinate Dishes: Organize a list of dishes to ensure
various options. Communicate with participants to avoid
duplicate dishes and create a balanced meal.

Consider Dietary Preferences: When signing up for potluck
items, ask participants to indicate any dietary restrictions or
preferences. This ensures that everyone can enjoy the dishes
without concerns.

Provide Serving Utensils: Remind participants to bring
serving utensils for their dishes. This ensures that everyone
can easily access and enjoy the potluck offerings.

Create a Sign-Up Sheet: Use a sign-up sheet to track who's
bringing what. This helps avoid last-minute surprises and
allows for any necessary adjustments.

Communicate Clearly: Clearly communicate the potluck
event's date, time, and location. Additionally, provide guidelines or themes to ensure a cohesive and enjoyable meal.

Plan for Allergies: Be mindful of allergies. Encourage participants to label their dishes with ingredients, especially if
common allergens exist.

Express Appreciation: Finally, thank each participant for their contribution. Expressing appreciation creates a positive atmosphere and makes everyone feel valued.

Showing Appreciation to Event Hosts and Organizers

Hosting events and coordinating activities take effort, and showing appreciation to hosts and organizers is a thoughtful gesture:

Express Gratitude Verbally: A simple "thank you" goes a long way. To acknowledge the host's efforts, express your gratitude verbally during or after the event.

Send a Thank-You Note: Consider sending a handwritten or digital thank-you note highlighting what you enjoyed or found well-organized about the event.

Bring a Host Gift: If you're attending an event at someone's home, bringing a small gift, such as flowers, wine, or a thoughtful item, is a lovely gesture of appreciation.

Offer to Help: Offer assistance before, during, or after the event. Your willingness to contribute to setup, cleanup, or coordination is a valuable form of gratitude.

Share Positive Feedback: Share positive feedback with others who attended the event. Recognizing the host's efforts publicly reinforces the value of their work.

Donate to a Cause: If you know of a cause the host supports, consider donating as a meaningful way to show appreciation and contribute to something important to them.

Follow-up: Follow up with a message expressing gratitude once again after the event. This reinforces your appreciation and leaves a positive and lasting impression.

By following these guidelines, you can confidently navigate group social events, manage group dinners and potluck gatherings, and show appreciation to hosts and organizers with consideration and tact. These practices create a positive and harmonious social environment, making every social event a memorable and enjoyable experience."

Meeting Someone's Parents for the First Time

Prepare for the Occasion: Before meeting someone's parents, it's helpful to learn about their background and interests from your partner or friend. This can provide you with conversation topics and make a positive impression.

Dress Appropriately: Dressing well shows respect for the occasion and your hosts. It's usually a good idea to choose an outfit that's slightly more formal than what you'd wear in a casual setting.

Arrive on Time: Punctuality is crucial. Arriving on time demonstrates your reliability and respect for their schedule. If you anticipate being late, inform your partner or friend so they can relay the message.

Be Polite and Respectful: Always be polite and respectful to your host's parents. Address them by their titles (Mr. or Mrs.) unless they invite you to use their first names. Maintain good eye contact and offer a firm handshake when meeting them.

Engage in Conversation: Engage in friendly conversation to get to know them better. Ask about their interests, hobbies, and experiences. Be an active listener, showing genuine interest in what they say.

Avoid Controversial Topics: Steer clear of controversial or sensitive topics such as politics, religion, or personal matters. Keep the conversation light and positive.

Show Appreciation: Express gratitude for their hospitality and the opportunity to meet them. A simple "Thank you for having me" goes a long way in showing your appreciation.

Job Interviews

Research the Company: Before the interview, research the company thoroughly. Understand its mission, values, products, and services. This knowledge will help you tailor your responses during the interview.

Dress Professionally: Dress appropriately for the industry and company culture. When in doubt, it's better to be slightly overdressed than underdressed. A neat and professional appearance makes a strong first impression.

Arrive Early: Aim to arrive at the interview location about 10-15 minutes early. This demonstrates punctuality and gives you time to compose yourself before the interview.

Bring Necessary Documents: Carry multiple copies of your resume, a list of references, and any other relevant documents the employer may require. Having these readily available shows preparedness.

Practice Common Interview Questions: Prepare for common interview questions by practicing your responses. Focus on highlighting your skills, experiences, and how they align with the job requirements.

Ask Questions: Prepare thoughtful questions to ask the interviewer. This demonstrates your interest in the role and the company. Avoid asking questions about salary or benefits in the initial interview.

Body Language: Maintain positive body language throughout the interview. Offer a firm handshake, maintain eye contact, and sit up straight. Avoid fidgeting or appearing overly nervous.

Follow-Up: Send a thank-you email within 24 hours of the interview to express your appreciation for the opportunity and reiterate your interest in the position.

Sporting Events

Know the Rules and Teams: If you're attending a sporting event, familiarize yourself with the rules of the game and the teams that are playing. This will enhance your enjoyment and participation.

Respect Spectator Etiquette: Follow the spectator etiquette of the sport you're watching. This may include standing during certain moments, keeping noise levels appropriate, and refraining from disruptive behavior.

Cheer Responsibly: It's fine to cheer for your favorite team, but do so in a respectful manner. Avoid derogatory or offensive language directed at opposing teams or fans.

Respect Personal Space: Be mindful of personal space when seated in crowded areas. Avoid blocking others' views and allow them to enjoy the game.

Stay Safe: Follow safety guidelines provided by the venue. If attending with children, keep them under supervision and ensure their safety.

Clean Up After Yourself: Dispose of trash properly and keep the seating area clean. Leaving a mess is discourteous to others and the venue staff.

Engage in Friendly Banter: Good-natured banter with fans of the opposing team can be fun, but avoid confrontational or aggressive behavior. Remember, it's all in the spirit of the game.

Enjoy the Experience: Finally, remember that attending a sporting event is about having a good time. Enjoy the experience and savor the moments, win or lose.

Mastering Etiquette in Diverse Scenarios

In our social lives, we often find ourselves in unique and diverse etiquette scenarios, ranging from special occasions to unconventional situations. Navigating these scenarios gracefully requires thoughtfulness and understanding. Here's a comprehensive guide to etiquette in various scenarios, offering context and clarity to ensure your actions align with good manners.

Etiquette for Special Occasions

Weddings

- **RSVP Timely:** Respond to wedding invitations by the specified date.
- **Gifts:** If available, bring or send a gift even if you cannot attend, following the couple's registry.
- **Behavior:** During ceremonies and speeches, show respect and avoid excessive use of mobile devices.

Birthdays

- **Gifts:** Choose a thoughtful gift based on the recipient's preferences.
- **RSVP:** Promptly respond to birthday invitations.
- **Acknowledgment:** Express your gratitude for birthday gifts with a thank-you note or message.

Other Special Occasions

- **Anniversaries, Graduations, etc.:** Mark milestones with a thoughtful card or small gift as a sign of appreciation.

The Importance of Tipping in Service Industries

Understanding the ins and outs of tipping etiquette is a valuable skill as you navigate various service scenarios. Tipping is not just about courtesy; it's a way to express appreciation for the quality of service provided and ensure fair compensation in service industries. Whether you're dining out, using transportation services, enjoying spa treatments, or receiving services at home, knowing when and how to tip appropriately is essential. Let's explore why tipping matters and understand the specifics of tipping guidelines in different contexts.

Tipping Etiquette

Tipping serves several vital purposes:

Recognition of Service: Tipping serves as a tangible expression of gratitude and recognition for the dedication and quality of service provided by individuals in service industries. It's a way of saying "thank you" beyond just words.

Supplementing Income: In many professions within the service industry, like restaurants and salons, employees often rely on tips as a significant part of their income. Tipping ensures they receive fair compensation for their hard work.

Encouraging Excellence: Tipping is also a powerful motivator for service providers to excel in their roles. When they know their efforts are appreciated through tips, it encourages them to consistently deliver exceptional service and go the extra mile.

Cultural Norms: Tipping practices are deeply rooted in many cultures and are considered standard in various service sectors. Following local tipping customs not only shows respect for cultural traditions but also helps maintain social norms and expectations.

Tipping Guidelines for Various Services

Restaurants and Cafes: When dining in restaurants that offer table service, it's customary to tip between 15% and 20% of the total bill. Always check the bill for a service charge, as it might already be included.

Barbers and Salon Stylists: Tipping between 15% and 20% of the service cost is common practice in the beauty industry. Don't forget to tip shampoo assistants when appropriate.

Taxi Drivers: Tipping around 10% to 15% of the fare is the norm for taxi services. You might consider a higher tip for exceptional service or assistance with luggage.

Delivery Services: When receiving food or packages through delivery services, tipping between 10% and 20% of the total order is expected to appreciate the convenience and service provided.

Bartenders: It's common to tip bartenders $1 to $2 per drink or 15% to 20% of the total bill, especially in busy bars where bartenders work diligently to craft your beverages.

Valet Parking Attendants: Tipping $2 to $5 is generally suitable when using valet parking services, acknowledging their help in ensuring your vehicle's safe handling.

Masseuses and Spa Services: The standard guideline for tipping in spa settings is 15% to 20% of the service cost, though some establishments may include a service charge.

Wedding Services: Tipping is often expected for wedding services like photographers, musicians, and catering staff. Always refer to contracts and guidelines for each service provider to ensure you appreciate their hard work.

Delivery Services (Non-Food): When receiving non-food deliveries like furniture or appliances, tipping $5 to $10 per person is appreciated for the effort in safely transporting your items.

Handling Tipping When Receiving Home Services

Movers: Tipping each mover individually with a standard tip of $10 to $20 per mover for a service day is appropriate. For particularly challenging moves, consider a higher tip as a token of gratitude for their hard work.

Repair Services (Plumbers, Electricians): Tipping repair service providers $10 to $20 is thoughtful, especially for extensive work or exceptional effort in solving your household issues.

Landscapers and Gardeners: Tipping $20 to $50 per person at the end of the season or after a significant project is a common practice, recognizing the dedication they put into enhancing your outdoor space.

Cleaning Services: Tipping house cleaners 10% to 15% of the cleaning cost is appreciated, with adjustments based on the quality of service provided. It's a way to acknowledge their commitment to maintaining your living space.

Gratuities for Professional Services

Personal Trainers: While tipping personal trainers is optional, it can be a gesture of appreciation. Consider an amount often equivalent to one session's fee or a small gift to express your gratitude for their guidance and expertise.

Hair Stylists and Salon Services: When receiving additional services like washing hair or applying color, it's considerate to tip assistants $5 to $10 in addition to tipping for the salon services, recognizing their role in enhancing your salon experience.

Tutors and Coaches: Tipping for private tutors or coaches is optional but can be done as a token of appreciation, often equivalent to one session's fee, showing gratitude for their educational support and mentorship.

These are general tipping guidelines, and practices can vary depending on location, cultural norms, and personal preferences. Always take into account the quality of service when determining your tip amount. Tipping is a way to express gratitude, foster positive interactions, and acknowledge the hard work of those providing various services.

Gifting Etiquette for Holidays and Celebrations

Gift Exchanges: Clarify expectations for gift exchanges within social groups to ensure everyone is on the same page regarding gift-giving.

Hostess Gifts: Bring a small gift when attending holiday gatherings to express appreciation for the host's hospitality.

Holiday Cards: Use holiday cards to convey well wishes and sentiments to friends and loved ones during the holiday season.

App-Based Services

Ride-Sharing Services: Tip your driver through the app or with cash after a ride to appreciate their service and safe transportation.

Food Delivery: Consider tipping delivery drivers through the app or cash upon delivery as a token of gratitude for the convenience of having food delivered to your doorstep.

Service Ratings: Provide ratings and feedback to support service providers based on your experience, helping others make informed decisions.

Digital Transactions

E-Gifts: Show appreciation for online services with digital gift cards or e-gifts, making it easy to express gratitude for exceptional service.

Virtual Tips: Some platforms allow virtual tipping, a convenient way to express gratitude for exceptional service and support content creators or service providers.

Subscription Services

Cancellation Etiquette: Offer timely notice when canceling subscription services to help providers manage their business effectively and reduce any inconveniences.

Online Collaborations

Virtual Meetings: Practice good etiquette by muting your microphone when not speaking, dressing professionally, and minimizing background noise to ensure productive and respectful virtual interactions.

General Tips for Uncommon Situations

Research Local Customs: When in doubt about tipping or showing appreciation, research local customs to align with cultural norms and avoid unintentional misunderstandings.

Ask for Guidance: Don't hesitate to ask service providers or hosts about tipping practices or expectations if you are uncertain, ensuring your gestures are well-received and appropriate.

Consider Personal Relationships: Gauge the strength of your relationship with service providers when determining the appropriate level of tipping or showing appreciation to ensure your gestures are heartfelt and meaningful.

Express Gratitude: Regardless of the situation, expressing gratitude verbally or through a thank-you note amplifies the impact of your gesture and fosters goodwill in various social and service-related contexts.

Travel Etiquette: Navigating the Journey with Grace

Traveling is an adventure that takes us through various settings, from bustling airports to cozy hotels and unique vacation rentals. Ensuring a smooth and enjoyable experience for everyone involved requires understanding and practicing travel etiquette. This section will explore airport and travel etiquette, hotel and accommodation tipping, the art of tipping tour guides, and etiquette for staying in vacation rentals.

Airport and Travel Etiquette

Prepare for Security Checks:

- Remove items from your pockets and place them in the provided bins.
- Place liquids in a clear, quart-sized bag as per the regulations.
- Show respect for the space and privacy of fellow travelers while waiting in line and during security screening.

During Security Checks:

- Cooperate fully with security checks at airports.
- Be prepared to remove your shoes, belts, and items from your pockets.
- Follow instructions from security personnel diligently.

- Maintain a respectful demeanor throughout the security process.

Boarding Etiquette: Maintain order during boarding by adhering to designated boarding groups. Pay attention to the size of your carry-on and efficiently stow it in the overhead bin.

Seat Reclining: If your seat reclines, gradually consider the space behind you. Avoid reclining during meal service, and be attentive to the comfort of the person behind you.

In-Flight Courtesy:

- Mind noise levels, especially on nighttime flights.
- Use headphones when watching movies or listening to music.
- Refrain from using strong scents and be considerate of personal space.

Deplaning Etiquette: Wait your turn to deplane, following the row-by-row process. Exercise patience and allow those before you to exit the aircraft first.

Patience and Kindness: Recognize that travel can be stressful. Cultivate patience and extend kindness to fellow travelers, airport staff, and airline personnel. A positive attitude contributes to a more pleasant journey for everyone.

Tipping in Hotels and While Traveling

When it comes to tipping in hotels and during your travels,

it's essential to understand the customs and practices to ensure a positive experience:

Housekeeping: Leaving a daily tip for housekeeping staff is a considerate gesture. You can choose to tip daily or at the end of your stay. Placing the tip in an envelope along with a note expressing your gratitude is a thoughtful touch.

Bellhops and Porters: When bellhops or porters assist with your luggage, it's customary to tip them between $2 to $5 per bag. The amount can vary based on the level of service they provide.

Concierge Services: Tipping for concierge services is discretionary but appreciated, especially if the concierge goes above and beyond to assist you. A tip ranging from $5 to $10 is appropriate for their efforts.

Room Service: When ordering room service, check your bill for any included service charges. If service charges are not included, consider leaving a 15% to 20% tip for the delivery.

Valet Parking Attendants: Tipping valet parking attendants is standard practice. When they return your car, it's customary to tip them between $2 to $5. Additional tips may be given for exceptional service.

Spa Services: Tipping for spa services can vary, so it's advisable to check if a service charge is already included. If not, a tip ranging from 15% to 20% of the service cost is customary.

Tipping Tour Guides and Local Services During Travel

Tour Guides: Show appreciation for tour guides by tipping them 10% to 15% of the tour cost. This amount can be adjusted based on the quality of the tour and the guide's expertise.

Local Transportation: When utilizing local drivers such as taxi drivers or rideshare services, tip according to local customs. Always check if a service charge is included in your fare.

Airport and Hotel Shuttle Drivers: When using shuttle services provided by hotels or airports, a tip of $2 to $5 per person is generally suitable.

Restaurant Service: Tipping in restaurants while traveling can vary widely by country. Before dining out, research the tipping norms at your travel destination to ensure that you tip appropriately.

These tipping practices can vary based on location, cultural norms, and personal preferences. Always consider the quality of service when determining your tip amount, and express your gratitude for the hard work of those providing various services during your travels.

Etiquette for Staying in Vacation Rentals

Communication with Hosts: Maintain clear and prompt communication with your hosts. Inform them of your arrival time and any special requests or requirements you may have.

Respect House Rules: Adhere to the house rules established by your host. These may include guidelines related to noise levels, smoking policies, and other considerations aimed at ensuring a harmonious stay.

Cleanliness:

1. Treat the vacation rental as you would your own space.
2. Leave it in the same or better condition than you found it.
3. Clean up after yourself and follow any specific instructions provided by the host.

Security and Privacy: Respect the security and privacy of the vacation rental. Always lock doors and windows when leaving, and avoid disturbing neighbors or fellow guests.

Check-Out Procedures: Follow the check-out procedures outlined by the host. This may include stripping beds, removing trash, or turning off appliances before departing.

Communication about Issues: If you encounter any issues during your stay, communicate with the host promptly and professionally. They can address concerns and ensure a more comfortable experience for you and future guests.

Review Thoughtfully: Leave a thoughtful and honest review for the vacation rental after your stay. Highlight positive aspects of your experience and provide constructive feedback, if necessary.

By adhering to these travel etiquette guidelines, you can navigate various travel settings with confidence and consideration for others. Practicing good travel etiquette enhances your journey, whether at the airport, staying in a hotel, exploring with a tour guide, or enjoying a vacation rental. It contributes to a positive travel experience for all.

Key Takeaways

Etiquette is About Respect and Consideration: Etiquette goes beyond rules; it's a way to show respect, consideration, and appreciation for others in various situations. Whether it's attending events, navigating unique scenarios, or engaging in the digital world, etiquette is your guide to positive interactions.

Effective Communication Strengthens Connections: Good etiquette includes responding to invitations and expressing gratitude, which helps strengthen connections with others. Be adaptable, as etiquette norms differ widely, and always be open to learning. Gratitude should be a constant companion, acknowledging acts of kindness and assistance.

Responsible and Thoughtful Actions Have Impact: Your responsible and thoughtful actions, like tipping service providers or respecting house rules, leave a lasting impact on those around you. Etiquette evolves with societal changes, so continue refining your skills as you grow. Embrace these principles to navigate life's intricate social tapestry with confidence and grace, making a positive impression on those you encounter.

Etiquette is a Lifelong Journey: Remember that etiquette is a lifelong journey. As society changes, so do etiquette norms. Stay open to evolving etiquette practices and adapt accordingly. Embracing these principles will empower you to navigate various social situations with poise and leave a positive mark on the people you meet.

Test Your Knowledge

1. What is one key purpose of etiquette in various scenarios?

- a. Following strict rules
- b. Demonstrating respect and consideration
- c. Showing off your knowledge
- d. Being the center of attention

2. When attending a wedding, what are the proper etiquette guidelines to follow?

- a. Ignore the invitation if you can't attend
- b. Bring a gift even if you can't attend
- c. Talk loudly during the ceremony
- d. Use your mobile phone to take pictures during speeches

3. Why is tipping for dining, deliveries, and personal care important in various cultures and industries?

- a. It helps service providers earn a fair income.
- b. It encourages exceptional service.
- c. It aligns with cultural norms.
- d. All of the above

4. What should you do when meeting someone's parents for the first time?

- a. Dress appropriately for the occasion.
- b. Be polite and use proper manners.
- c. Bring a small gift or token of appreciation.
- d. All of the above.

5. How can you express gratitude to service providers who offer exceptional service in the digital realm?

- a. Ignore their efforts
- b. Give them a low rating
- c. Provide virtual tips or positive feedback
- d. Complain about minor issues

4 FINANCIAL LITERACY

Financial literacy is a crucial skill, especially as you embark on a new chapter in your life. Take Brooklyn's story, for example. She had just moved out of her parents' house and was thrilled with her newfound independence. However, she was spending her money before taking care of her bills.

With her income stretched thin, Brooklyn found herself constantly behind on bills and struggling to make ends meet. Her plans to enjoy her newfound freedom turned into a constant battle with financial stress and constraints.

It was a wake-up call for Brooklyn. She realized the importance of financial literacy in managing her money effectively, saving for emergencies, and still having funds for fun. Determined to take control of her finances, she knew that financial literacy was her ticket to financial security, peace of mind, and the freedom to enjoy her independence without money worries.

Now that you've heard Brooklyn's financial journey, you might be wondering, "What exactly is financial literacy, and how can it help me avoid similar pitfalls?"

In this chapter, we'll delve deeper into the world of financial literacy. We'll explore what it means to be financially literate, why it's crucial for your future, and how it empowers you to make informed and responsible financial decisions. You'll discover practical aspects of managing your money, including budgeting, saving, and planning for a secure financial future.

Financial literacy isn't just about numbers and budgets; it's about gaining the knowledge and skills to navigate the complexities of personal finance successfully. So, if you want to avoid financial stress, achieve your goals, and relish the freedom that financial security brings, let's embark on this exciting journey of financial literacy. It's your key to unlocking a brighter and more secure future.

Budgeting and Money Management

Budgeting is a fundamental aspect of effective money management. It involves creating a plan for allocating your income to cover expenses, save, and achieve financial goals. Let's dive into personal finance, a topic of immense importance for young adults like you. Financial literacy is all about equipping yourself with the skills to make informed and responsible financial decisions, and it's never too early to start.

Creating a Personal Budget & Its Importance

A personal budget is like your financial GPS, mapping out your expected income and guiding you on allocating funds for various expenses, savings, and financial goals.

Here's how to get started:

Assess Your Income: Take a close look at all the money coming your way, whether it's your regular salary, income from a part-time job, or any other sources like freelancing or investments. Understanding your total income is the first step to managing your finances effectively. It allows you to see the full picture of what you have to work with each month.

List Your Expenses: Divide your expenses into two main categories: fixed and variable. Fixed expenses are the stable, recurring costs in your life, such as rent or mortgage payments, utility bills, and insurance premiums. On the other hand, variable expenses are the more flexible costs that can change from month to month, like dining out, entertainment, or shopping for clothes. This categorization helps you see where your money is consistently allocated and where it might fluctuate.

Identify Financial Goals: Take some time to think about your financial aspirations. What are your short-term goals, such as building an emergency fund or saving for a vacation?

Equally important are your long-term goals, like planning for retirement or buying a home. Defining your goals gives you a clear direction and purpose for your financial decisions.

Allocate Funds: Once you've determined your income, listed your expenses, and identified your financial goals, it's time to create a plan. Allocate your income to different categories based on your priorities. This includes deciding how much you'll allocate for essentials like groceries, utilities, rent or mortgage, and transportation. Don't forget to allocate funds toward your savings goals as well. The key is to strike a balance between covering your needs and progressing toward your financial objectives without exceeding your income. This step ensures that you're actively working towards your goals and maintaining financial stability.

The importance of this budgeting exercise cannot be overstated:

Financial Awareness: Creating a budget shines a spotlight on where your money is going, providing you with a clear and honest view of your spending habits. This awareness is the first step in making informed financial decisions and identifying areas where you can cut back or make adjustments.

Goal Setting: Budgeting is a powerful tool for setting and achieving financial goals. Whether it's saving for a dream vacation, buying a new car, or building an emergency fund, a well-structured budget allows you to allocate resources strategically, making your financial aspirations more attainable.

Expense Control: One of the primary benefits of budgeting is that it puts you in the driver's seat when it comes to controlling your spending. With a budget in place, you can track your expenses and ensure that you're not overspending in any particular category. This control is essential for maintaining financial stability and avoiding unnecessary debt.

Emergency Preparedness: A comprehensive budget includes provisions for an emergency fund and a financial safety net. These funds are crucial for covering unexpected expenses, such as medical bills or car repairs, without derailing your overall financial plan. Budgeting ensures that you are prepared for life's uncertainties.

Debt Reduction: If you're dealing with debt, budgeting is an invaluable tool for developing a structured plan to pay it down. By allocating a portion of your income to debt repayment while still covering essential expenses, you can make steady progress towards becoming debt-free. Budgeting provides a roadmap for achieving financial freedom.

By following these steps and creating a personal budget, you'll be well on your way to mastering your finances, gaining control over your money, and achieving your financial goals. It's a practical and empowering skill that can lead to a more secure and prosperous future.

Fixed vs. Variable Expenses

Understanding the distinction between fixed and variable expenses is essential for effective budgeting and financial planning:

Fixed Expenses: Fixed expenses are the bedrock of your budget, representing consistent and predictable costs that remain relatively stable from month to month. These expenses are typically non-negotiable and include essential obligations such as:

- **Rent or Mortgage Payments:** Your monthly housing costs, whether you rent or own a home, are a prime example of a fixed expense. The amount you owe remains consistent unless you have a lease or mortgage rate adjustment.
- **Utilities:** Essential services like electricity, gas, water, and internet fall under fixed expenses. While the specific amounts might fluctuate slightly with usage, they are generally predictable.
- **Loan Payments:** If you have student loans, a car loan, or a mortgage, the monthly repayments constitute fixed expenses. These payments have predetermined amounts and due dates.
- **Insurance Premiums:** Monthly insurance premiums for health, auto, or renters' insurance are typically fixed. You'll know the exact amount you need to pay each month to maintain coverage.

Variable Expenses: Variable expenses, on the other hand, are more flexible and can vary significantly from one month to the next. These expenses encompass discretionary spending and lifestyle choices, including:

- **Groceries:** While groceries are a necessity, the amount you spend can fluctuate based on your meal planning, shopping habits, and dietary choices.
- **Dining Out:** Expenses related to dining at restaurants, cafes, or ordering takeout fall into the variable category. These costs can vary depending on your social activities and dining preferences.
- **Entertainment:** Variable expenses encompass entertainment activities such as going to the movies, attending concerts, or subscribing to streaming services beyond your fixed subscriptions.
- **Travel:** Any expenses related to travel, whether it's a weekend getaway or a vacation, are variable. Travel costs can vary widely based on the destination and the activities you choose.
- **Shopping and Personal Expenses:** Non-essential purchases, such as clothing, electronics, or personal grooming, are considered variable expenses. Your spending in this category depends on your wants and needs.

Understanding the difference between fixed and variable expenses is crucial for effective budgeting. Fixed expenses provide a stable foundation, while variable expenses offer flexibility. By categorizing your expenses in this way, you can prioritize essential financial obligations, allocate funds for savings and debt repayment, and make informed decisions about discretionary spending based on your financial goals and priorities.

Knowing how to manage both types is crucial for a balanced budget. Fixed expenses are non-negotiable, but with variable expenses, you have room for adjustments to align with your financial goals.

Mastering Your Spending Habits

Analyzing Expense Categories: To gain a comprehensive insight into your spending patterns, break down your expenses into distinct categories, such as groceries, dining out, entertainment, and utilities. This meticulous categorization provides a detailed understanding of precisely where your money is being allocated.

Setting Limits and Allocating Your Budget: Promote financial discipline by allocating specific amounts to different spending categories according to your financial goals and priorities. Setting spending limits not only fosters responsible budgeting but also assists in curbing unnecessary expenses that may hinder your financial progress.

Adjusting Spending Habits for Financial Alignment: Flexibility is key to financial success. Identify areas where your spending habits can be adjusted to better align with your financial goals. This could involve making conscious efforts to reduce discretionary spending or seeking more cost-effective alternatives for certain expenditures.

Prioritizing Essential Needs Over Non-Essential Wants: Conduct a critical assessment of your expenses by distinguishing between needs and wants. Prioritize fulfilling essential needs while maintaining mindfulness regarding discretionary spending on non-essential wants. This practice ensures that you allocate your resources thoughtfully and in alignment with your financial objectives.

Integrating Financial Goals with Budgeting

Let's put your financial goals on the map of your budget.

Spread the Wealth: Allocate specific portions of your budget to different financial goals, ensuring that your hard-earned money goes where it matters most.

Regular Review: Life isn't static, and neither are your goals. Review and adjust your budget allocations periodically based on evolving circumstances, income fluctuations, and changing financial objectives.

Priority Alert: Don't forget the golden rule of budgeting – your emergency fund is your safety net, so make it a priority.

The Necessity of an Emergency Fund

An emergency fund is like a financial safety net, providing you with a buffer against unexpected expenses or financial setbacks. Here's why it's crucial:

Financial Security: An emergency fund offers financial security, reducing stress and anxiety during challenging times. It prevents you from relying on credit cards or loans to cover unforeseen costs.

Unpredictable Emergencies: Life is full of surprises, and many situations can't be foreseen. Emergencies could include medical expenses, car repairs, home repairs, or sudden job loss. Having an emergency fund means you're prepared for these unexpected events.

Defining a Genuine Financial Emergency

Not all unexpected expenses qualify as genuine financial emergencies. It's essential to differentiate between true emergencies and regular, albeit unexpected, costs:

Genuine Emergencies: These are unforeseen and necessary expenses that, if left unaddressed, could have severe consequences. Examples include medical emergencies, urgent home repairs (e.g., a leaking roof), or unexpected job loss.

Non-Emergencies: Regular, irregular, or optional expenses, like car maintenance, vacations, or holiday shopping, are not genuine emergencies. While they may be unexpected, they can be budgeted for separately.

Determining the Right Amount for Your Emergency Fund

The size of your emergency fund depends on your individual circumstances, but there are some general guidelines to consider. To get you started, aim to save at least $1000 to always have available at your disposal.

Basic Starter Emergency Fund: Financial experts often recommend starting with a basic emergency fund that covers essential living expenses for three to six months. This includes rent or mortgage, utilities, groceries, transportation, and insurance premiums. Having this fund in place provides a good foundation for financial stability.

Building a Solid Emergency Fund: Over time, aim to build your emergency fund to cover living expenses for six to nine months or even up to one year. This extended cushion offers added peace of mind and protection against more prolonged financial challenges, such as extended unemployment.

Consider Personal Factors: Adjust the size of your emergency fund based on your specific situation. Factors like job stability, health, and family circumstances may influence the amount you need. For example, those with irregular income or dependents may want a larger fund.

Savings Milestones: You don't need to save the full amount all at once. Set milestones and gradually work towards your goal. Even having a small emergency fund initially is better than none at all.

In summary, an emergency fund is a financial lifeline that provides stability and peace of mind during unexpected situations. It's crucial to distinguish between real emergencies and regular expenses and save an amount that aligns with your unique financial situation and goals. Building a solid emergency fund is a fundamental step toward financial security and resilience.

Side Hustles and Additional Income

In today's dynamic world, many individuals are turning to side hustles to boost their income and pursue their passions. Whether you're looking to pay off debt, save for a dream vacation, or simply increase your financial flexibility, side hustles offer a valuable opportunity to amplify your earnings. In this chapter, we'll explore the ins and outs of side hustles, from identifying your skills and interests to effectively managing your time and resources, helping you embark on a successful journey toward financial growth and fulfillment.

Recognizing Your Income Potential

If you're eager to boost your income, you can tap into your unique skills, hobbies, and passions. Here's how to get started:

Identifying Your Strengths and Interests

What Are You Good At?: Begin by assessing your strengths and skills. Identify areas where you excel, whether it's teaching, writing, crafting, or a particular hobby. Your innate talents can be the foundation for a successful side hustle.

Passion Projects: Beyond your skills, consider what you're passionate about. Pursuing a side hustle related to your interests can be fulfilling and motivating. It can also help you stay committed and enjoy the journey.

Market Research and Positioning

Market Savvy: Before diving in, research the demand for your chosen side hustle in your local area or online marketplaces. Understanding market needs and competition will help you position your services effectively. Look for gaps in the market or ways to differentiate yourself.

Time Management and Flexibility

Time Check: Assess how much time you can realistically dedicate to your side hustle. It's crucial to strike a balance between your primary job, personal life, and your new income-generating endeavor. Flexibility is essential, as it allows you to adapt to changing circumstances.

Exploring Side Hustle Ideas

Inspiration Station: The world of side hustles is vast and diverse. Explore a range of ideas, from dog walking to tutoring, freelancing in various fields, or selling handmade crafts. The key is to find an option that resonates with you and aligns with your skills and interests.

Evaluate Viability: While brainstorming ideas, evaluate their viability and income potential. Consider factors like startup costs, required equipment or resources, and the potential return on investment. Some side hustles may require minimal upfront expenses, making them more accessible.

Starting Small and Scaling

Begin Small: It's okay to start small with your side hustle. Begin by offering your services to friends and family or on a small scale. This allows you to refine your offerings, gain experience, and build a client base gradually.

Scaling Up: As your side hustle gains traction and you become more comfortable, explore opportunities to scale up your business. This might involve increasing your client base, expanding your services, or investing in marketing to reach a broader audience.

Financial Planning and Goals

Set Financial Goals: Clearly define your financial goals for your side hustle. Whether it's paying off debt, building an emergency fund, or saving for a specific purpose, having clear objectives will keep you motivated.

Budget and Taxes: Keep track of your side hustle income and expenses to ensure you're financially responsible. Understand the tax implications of your side hustle and plan accordingly.

Remember that starting a side hustle requires dedication, effort, and a willingness to learn. It's an opportunity to not only increase your income but also explore your passions and interests while enhancing your financial well-being.

Balancing Your Checkbook and Avoiding Overdrafts

Balancing your checkbook is a fundamental practice in personal finance that forms the bedrock of financial accuracy and stability. This section explores why balancing your checkbook matters, walks you through a step-by-step guide, introduces useful tools and apps, and delves into critical aspects of responsible checking account management.

Why Balance Your Checkbook?

Balancing your checkbook is a crucial financial practice for several reasons:

Accuracy and Awareness: Balancing your checkbook ensures that your recorded transactions align precisely with your bank's records, accurately representing your available funds. It's akin to a financial reality check.

Detecting Errors: Beyond mere accuracy, regular reconciliation of your checkbook helps you become your financial detective. It's your means of identifying any discrepancies or errors in your financial transactions, enabling you to address and correct them promptly.

Preventing Overdrafts: Overdrafts are like financial potholes —they can cause a bumpy ride. You can avoid overdrawing your account by keeping an accurate account of your transactions. Overdrafts can result in fees and other unpleasant financial consequences, so avoiding them at all costs is wise.

Step-by-Step Guide to Balancing Your Checkbook

Record Transactions Promptly: A timely recording of all transactions is the foundation of a balanced checkbook. Whether it's checks, deposits, or debit card transactions, be diligent in entering them into your checkbook register as soon as they occur. This ensures accuracy and helps you stay aware of your spending in real-time.

Compare with Bank Statements: Regularly compare your checkbook register with your monthly bank statements. It's the financial equivalent of double-checking your homework. Verify that the transactions in both records match and are accurately reflected. If you spot discrepancies, don't fret; we'll address them shortly.

Reconcile Monthly: At the close of each month, it's time to reconcile your checkbook with your bank statement. This involves ensuring that your register's ending balance perfectly matches the statement's ending balance. The goal? A harmonious financial symphony.

Address Discrepancies: While rare, discrepancies can occasionally sneak in. If you discover differences between your records and the bank statement, don't ignore them. Investigate and resolve these issues promptly. It may involve reaching out to the bank or reviewing your receipts to pinpoint the source of the discrepancy.

Balancing Tools and Apps

Checkbook Register Apps: In our digital age, we have tools at our fingertips to make this process more convenient. Consider using digital checkbook register apps like Goodbudget, PocketGuard, or even dedicated banking apps offered by your financial institution. These apps simplify the input and tracking of transactions, allowing you to maintain financial accuracy.

Budgeting Software: Broaden your financial horizons by exploring budgeting software such as YNAB (You Need A Budget) or Mint. These versatile tools help track expenses and facilitate overall financial management, keeping your financial house in order.

Avoiding Overdrafts and Managing Your Checking Account

Overdraft fees are the stealthy financial predators that pounce when you spend more money than is available in your checking account. These fees can vary by bank but typically range from $30 to $40 or even more for each overdraft occurrence. When multiple transactions occur without sufficient funds, these fees can add up quickly, leading to significant unexpected expenses.

Tips for Avoiding Overdrafts:

- **Regularly Check Your Balance:** Staying informed about your account balance is your financial compass, guiding you away from rocky financial waters. Make it a habit to check your balance regularly, whether through your bank's website, mobile app, or ATMs.
- **Set Up Alerts:** Take advantage of modern banking features that allow you to stay vigilant effortlessly. Enable account alerts that notify you when your balance drops below a specified threshold. These alerts act like a financial guardian angel on your shoulder, giving you timely warnings to avoid overdrafts.
- **Opt-Out of Overdraft Protection:** While it may sound counterintuitive, consider opting out of overdraft protection. This option prevents transactions that exceed your balance from going through, acting as a safety net to prevent costly missteps. Without overdraft protection, if you attempt a transaction with insufficient funds, it will

be declined rather than processed with an overdraft fee.

Managing Overdraft Protection: It's important to note that if you have overdraft protection, it's not a free pass. Overdraft protection typically means that your bank covers the transaction temporarily, allowing it to go through even if you don't have enough funds. However, you'll need to pay back the overdraft amount promptly. This means that you'll need to bring your account balance back to a positive level, often within a short time frame, to avoid additional fees and potential account closure.

By being aware of the costs associated with overdrafts, monitoring your account balance, setting up alerts, and making informed decisions about overdraft protection, you can effectively manage your checking account and avoid unnecessary expenses.

Managing Your Checking Account Responsibly

Managing Your Checking Account Responsibly

Managing your checking account effectively involves not only balancing your checkbook but also understanding the various ways to pay your bills. Let's explore different payment methods and their pros and cons:

Automatic Payments (Auto Withdrawals):

Pros:

- Convenience: Set it and forget it. Automatic payments save time and ensure bills are paid on time.
- Timely Payments: Eliminates the risk of late payments and associated fees.
- Consistency: Payments are made regularly, helping you maintain a positive payment history.

Cons:

- Lack of Control: Auto withdrawals can become a blind spot if not monitored. You may overlook changes in billing amounts or unauthorized charges.
- Overdraft Risk: Until you're financially literate, auto withdrawals can be risky, potentially leading to overdrafts if you forget to account for them.

Manual Payments (Writing Checks or Online Payments):

Pros:

- Control: You have complete control over when and how much you pay.
- Awareness: Manual payments require you to actively engage with your finances, promoting financial awareness.

- Flexibility: You can adjust payment amounts based on your financial situation.

Cons:

- Time-Consuming: Manual payments can be more time-consuming than automatic ones.
- Potential for Late Payments: If not managed well, manual payments may lead to late fees.

Paying by Phone:

Pros:

- Convenience: Paying by phone offers flexibility and convenience.
- Immediate Confirmation: You receive immediate confirmation of your payment.

Cons:

- Security Risks: Phone payments can pose security risks if not done through secure channels.
- May Incur Service Fees: Some service providers may charge convenience fees for phone payments.

Additional Tips for Managing Your Checking Account Responsibly:

Monitor Automatic Payments: While automatic payments are convenient, keep a watchful eye on these transactions to avoid unexpected deductions.

Review Statements: Regularly reviewing your bank statements is a prudent practice. It helps you promptly catch any unauthorized transactions or errors, giving you the power to rectify them.

Secure Personal Information: In this age of digital transactions, safeguarding your checkbook, debit card, and personal information is vital. These safeguards prevent fraud and ensure your financial security.

By understanding the pros and cons of different payment methods and adopting responsible practices, you'll not only balance your checkbook but also balance your financial life, taking steps toward stability, accuracy, and peace of mind.

The Importance of an Emergency Credit Card

In life's unpredictable journey, unexpected expenses like medical emergencies, car repairs, or urgent home fixes can catch us off guard. An emergency credit card serves as your reliable financial safety net, offering unparalleled convenience when immediate cash is unavailable. Beyond convenience, responsible use of such a card also helps build a strong credit history, a vital foundation for future financial endeavors.

Obtaining and Managing an Emergency Credit Card

Choosing the Right Card: When navigating the world of credit cards, remember that one size doesn't fit all. It's crucial to select a credit card that suits your specific financial needs and creditworthiness. Hunt for a card that offers favorable terms, low interest rates, and minimal fees. Much like choosing the perfect tool for a job, this decision can significantly impact your financial stability.

Credit Limit Considerations: Your credit limit plays a pivotal role in your financial safety net. Ensure it's set at a level that can adequately cover potential emergency expenses, but exercise caution not to overextend yourself. Finding that sweet spot where your credit limit aligns with your repayment capacity is essential for responsible credit card use.

Read the Terms and Conditions: The fine print holds the key to understanding your credit card agreement. Dive into the terms and conditions, scrutinizing interest rates, fees, and any rewards or benefits tied to the card. Knowledge is your financial armor, empowering you to make informed decisions and avoid potential pitfalls.

Using Sparingly: While your emergency credit card can be a lifeline during unexpected financial crises, it's important to adhere to the golden rule: reserve it for genuine emergencies, not everyday expenses or discretionary spending. Remember, it's not an extra wallet but your financial safety rope, ready to support you when you need it most.

Making On-Time Payments and Responsible Usage

Responsible Credit Card Usage and Avoiding Debt: A credit card is a powerful financial tool, offering convenience, safety in emergencies, and potential rewards like cashback or travel points. However, it also carries the risk of debt if not used responsibly. The cardinal rule of credit card usage is to charge only what you can pay off in full each month, preventing the cycle of debt.

Importance of Full Payments: To avoid the debt trap, always aim to pay off your credit card balance entirely each month. This practice keeps you within your means and prevents interest charges from accumulating. Essentially, you're using your credit card as a financial tool rather than a source of long-term debt.

Avoiding Cash Advances and Monitoring Statements: Cash advances from your credit card can be like quicksand, easy to sink into and challenging to escape due to higher interest rates and additional fees. Reserve this option strictly for genuine emergencies. Regularly monitoring your credit card statements is essential; they serve as your financial mirror, reflecting your spending habits and account activity. This practice helps you stay informed about your spending and promptly identify any unauthorized transactions, acting as your financial GPS toward security and peace of mind.

Building and Maintaining Good Credit

Maintaining a consistent and responsible approach to credit card usage is essential for building a positive credit history, which acts as your financial passport. Strive for balance by keeping credit card balances low in relation to your credit limit, with a target credit utilization ratio below 30%. This demonstrates responsible credit use and strengthens your credit score. Furthermore, avoid closing old credit card accounts, as the length of your credit history significantly impacts your credit score. Think of these older accounts as financial elders, offering wisdom and stability to your credit profile.

Understanding Credit Scores, Debt, and Building Good Credit

Understanding Credit Scores: Credit scores are like your financial report card, influencing various aspects of your financial life. They are calculated using factors such as payment history, credit utilization, length of credit history, types of credit in use, and new credit applications. Taking the time to comprehend these factors can empower you to make informed decisions about your credit.

Managing Debt Responsibly: Responsible credit management is crucial for avoiding the pitfalls of excessive debt. Accumulating high levels of debt relative to your credit limit can negatively impact your credit score. Finding the right balance between credit utilization and debt management is key to maintaining a healthy financial profile.

Building Good Credit Habits: Cultivating good credit habits is akin to tending to a growing plant. It involves consistently paying bills on time, avoiding maxing out credit cards, and regularly reviewing your credit report for errors or discrepancies. These daily financial practices contribute to a positive credit history and a strong credit score, opening doors to various financial opportunities.

What is a Credit Score?

A credit score is your financial fingerprint—a numerical representation of your creditworthiness. It condenses your credit history and financial behavior into a three-digit number. Consider it a quick assessment for lenders, gauging your loan repayment likelihood.

Building and Maintaining Your Credit Score

Establishing Credit: If you're new to credit, it's essential to take deliberate steps to establish your credit history. This can be achieved by obtaining a credit card, securing a small loan, or becoming an authorized user on someone else's credit account. Think of it as laying the first brick in building your financial castle. These initial credit endeavors provide you with the opportunity to demonstrate your creditworthiness and begin constructing a robust financial profile that will serve you well in the future.

Timely Payments: The heartbeat of your credit score is punctual payments. To maintain a healthy credit history and boost your credit score, it's crucial to consistently pay all your bills, loans, and credit card payments on time. Timely payments not only establish a rhythm of financial responsibility but also reflect positively on your creditworthiness.

Credit Mix: Maintaining a diverse mix of credit types can have a positive impact on your credit score. This mix typically includes credit cards, installment loans (like auto loans or personal loans), and retail accounts (store credit cards). Demonstrating your ability to manage various types of credit responsibly showcases your financial versatility and can enhance your creditworthiness in the eyes of lenders.

Credit Utilization: Your credit utilization ratio plays a significant role in your credit score. To maintain a favorable credit utilization ratio, it's advisable to keep your credit card balances low relative to your credit limits. A low credit utilization ratio demonstrates your judicious use of available credit, indicating to creditors that you're not relying heavily on borrowed funds and are capable of managing your credit responsibly.

Key Takeaways

- **Budgeting is Key:** Establishing and sticking to a budget is the foundation of financial literacy. It provides the roadmap for managing your income, expenses, and savings.
- **Emergency Preparedness:** Building an emergency fund and having an emergency credit card are vital aspects of financial security. They offer protection and peace of mind during unforeseen circumstances.
- **Credit and Debt Management:** Responsible use of credit cards, understanding credit scores, and managing debt are essential for a healthy financial future. These practices pave the way for better financial opportunities.
- **Financial Goals Matter:** Setting clear financial goals and following the SMART criteria helps you prioritize and achieve your objectives. It ensures your resources are directed toward what matters most to you.
- **Protecting Your Financial Identity:** Safeguarding your personal and financial information, monitoring your credit, and being cautious online are crucial

steps to avoid identity theft and maintain financial stability.

By mastering these key principles of financial literacy, you'll be better equipped to make informed financial decisions, achieve your goals, and build a secure and prosperous future.

Test Your Knowledge

1. What is the primary purpose of creating a personal budget?

- a. To track your favorite TV shows
- b. To plan your vacation
- c. To manage your income and expenses
- d. To learn a new language

2. Why is it important to make on-time payments for your credit card bills?

- a. Because it's fun
- b. Because it impresses your friends
- c. Because it helps build and maintain a positive credit history
- d. Because it's required by law

3. What is the significance of an emergency fund?

- a. It acts as a vacation fund
- b. It provides a financial safety net for unexpected expenses
- c. It's a fund for luxury shopping
- d. It helps you invest in the stock market

4. Which of the following is NOT a factor that affects your credit score?

- a. Payment history
- b. Credit utilization
- c. Length of credit history
- d. Your favorite color

5. What is the recommended credit utilization ratio for maintaining a positive credit score?

- a. Over 50%
- b. Exactly 30%
- c. Below 30%
- d. It doesn't matter

6. Which of the following is NOT a step in balancing your checkbook?

- a. Recording all transactions promptly
- b. Avoiding checking your bank statements
- c. Comparing your checkbook register with your bank statements
- d. Reconciling your checkbook with your bank statement monthly

7. Which of the following is NOT a strategy for managing debt?

- a. Creating a structured repayment plan
- b. Prioritizing high-interest debts
- c. Negotiating with creditors
- d. Accumulating new debt regularly

5 INDEPENDENT LIVING

Imagine this: you're in control, making your own choices, and embracing the exciting challenges of life on your terms. Independent living is your chance to break free, but it comes with responsibilities, from managing your own space to handling your finances. This guide is your ticket to mastering the art of independent living and enjoying the freedom you've been waiting for.

Allow me to introduce you to Sarah, a young adult who recently embarked on her journey into independent living. Sarah was thrilled to move into her very own apartment, a place she had fallen in love with at first sight. It was spacious, in a great location, and had all the features she ever dreamed of. However, there was one tiny detail she hadn't fully considered: the cost.

Sarah soon realized that the apartment of her dreams came with a price tag that stretched her budget to its limits. Between rent, utilities, and other expenses, she found herself struggling to make ends meet. To make matters more challenging, her daily commute to work was about an hour each way, putting additional wear and tear on her car and increasing her fuel costs.

In the beginning, Sarah relied heavily on fast food for her meals due to her busy schedule and lack of cooking skills. But as the bills started piling up, she knew she needed to find a more cost-effective way to take care of herself.

With determination and a desire to master the art of independent living, Sarah decided to tackle her financial challenges head-on. She began by creating a budget to track her expenses and started learning how to cook simple, budget-friendly meals at home.

Sarah didn't stop there. She got clever with her commute and discovered that she had a coworker who lived not too far away. They decided to take turns commuting together, which not only saved Sarah money but also made her daily journey much more enjoyable.

By making these changes, Sarah was not only able to save money but also improve her overall well-being. She discovered that cooking her meals was not only cost-effective but also healthier and more satisfying.

When her lease finally came to an end, Sarah had learned valuable lessons about budgeting, the importance of making informed decisions when it came to housing, and the benefits of finding creative solutions to everyday challenges. She embarked on a new apartment hunt, this time with a more realistic budget in mind. She found a place that was the right size, at the right price, and still conveniently located.

Sarah's journey into independent living had its share of challenges, but it also taught her the importance of financial literacy, budgeting, and making choices that align with her goals and resources. As you read on, you'll gain insights into these essential life skills, helping you navigate your own path to independence with confidence and success.

Choosing the Right Place for You

Evaluate Your Finances: Take a thorough look at your financial situation, including income, savings, and monthly expenses. Determine the amount you can comfortably allocate to rent without compromising other essential needs.

Consider Additional Costs: Beyond rent, account for expenses like utilities, internet, groceries, and transportation. This comprehensive budgeting approach ensures you have a realistic understanding of your financial commitments.

The 30% Rule: A common guideline is to spend no more than 30% of your monthly income on rent. This helps maintain a healthy balance between housing costs and overall financial well-being.

Location

Proximity to Work or School: Choose a convenient location for commuting to work or school. Consider the time and cost associated with transportation.

Neighborhood Safety: Research the safety of potential neighborhoods. Online resources, local crime statistics, and talking to current residents can provide valuable insights.

Amenities and Services: Assess the proximity of essential services and amenities, such as grocery stores, medical facilities, public transportation, and recreational areas.

Community Vibes: Spend time in the neighborhood to feel its atmosphere. Consider your preferences regarding urban or suburban living, noise levels, and community activities.

Apartment Hunting Tips

Start your apartment search well in advance to have ample time for research and visits.

Use Online Platforms: Explore online rental platforms, real estate websites, and apps to browse available listings. These platforms often provide filters to refine your search based on preferences.

Attend Open Houses: Physically inspect potential apartments by attending open houses. This allows you to assess the condition of the property and its surroundings.

Bring a Checklist: Create a checklist of essential features and requirements. Use it during apartment visits to ensure that the property meets your criteria.

Ask Questions: Don't hesitate to ask the landlord or property manager questions about the lease, maintenance, and any specific concerns you may have.

Understanding Lease Agreements

Read Thoroughly: Carefully read the entire lease agreement before signing. Pay attention to clauses regarding rent, lease duration, maintenance responsibilities, and any penalties for breaking the lease.

Clarify Ambiguities: Seek clarification on any ambiguous or confusing terms within the lease. It's crucial to clearly understand your rights and obligations as a tenant.

Security Deposit Details: Understand the terms related to the security deposit, including the amount, conditions for its return, and any deductions that may be made.

Lease Duration: Confirm the duration of the lease and any provisions related to renewals or termination. Understand the penalties for breaking the lease early.

Document Property Condition: Document the property's current condition before moving in. Take photos or videos and make notes. This can be valuable when discussing security deposit refunds at the end of the lease.

Organizing and Maintaining Your Space

Declutter Regularly: Keeping your living space clutter-free isn't just about aesthetics; it also contributes to a more organized and peaceful environment. Regularly go through your belongings, and if you come across items you no longer need or use, consider donating or selling them. By doing this, you'll not only maintain a tidy living space but also free up valuable room for activities and storage.

Storage Solutions: Efficient storage is a game-changer in independent living. Invest in shelves, bins, and organizers to maximize your living space and keep your belongings neatly arranged. By having a designated place for everything, you'll reduce clutter and make it easier to find what you need when you need it.

Create a Cleaning Schedule: Establishing a cleaning schedule is a key part of adulting. It ensures that no corner of your home gets neglected. Create a routine that includes daily tasks like doing the dishes and tidying up, as well as weekly chores like vacuuming and dusting. Having a schedule helps you stay on top of housekeeping and maintain a clean and inviting living space.

Personalization: Your living space should reflect your personality and make you feel comfortable. Add personal touches through decor, artwork, or furnishings that resonate with you. Personalization not only enhances the aesthetics of your home but also contributes to your overall well-being by creating a space that feels uniquely yours.

Cleaning and Housekeeping Tips

Daily Maintenance: Incorporate daily cleaning habits into your routine. Simple tasks like washing dishes immediately after meals, wiping down surfaces, and making your bed each morning can go a long way in keeping your living space clean and organized. Consistency with these small tasks makes daily maintenance easier.

Weekly Cleaning: Designate specific days for deeper cleaning. On these days, focus on tasks like vacuuming, mopping, dusting, and cleaning the bathroom. Regular weekly cleaning prevents dirt and grime from building up and ensures a more hygienic environment.

Cleaning Supplies: Keep essential cleaning supplies readily available. Stock up on items like all-purpose cleaners, sponges, microfiber cloths, and trash bags. Having these supplies on hand ensures that you can quickly tackle cleaning tasks as they arise, making the process more efficient.

Home Repairs and Maintenance

Learn Basic Repairs: Basic home repair skills can save you time and money. Familiarize yourself with tasks like fixing a leaky faucet, changing light bulbs, and unclogging drains. Having these skills allows you to address common issues independently and avoid calling in professionals for minor repairs.

Create a Maintenance Calendar: Develop a maintenance

calendar to keep track of important tasks. This includes changing air filters, testing smoke detectors, and servicing appliances. Regular maintenance not only extends the lifespan of your home systems but also helps prevent major issues that can be costly to fix.

Emergency Preparedness: Being prepared for emergencies is a crucial aspect of independent living. Know how to shut off utilities like water and gas in case of emergencies. Keep a basic toolkit with essential tools for quick fixes. Additionally, have a list of emergency contacts readily available. Quick action during emergencies can minimize damage and ensure your safety.

Landlord Communication: Maintain open and prompt communication with your landlord regarding any necessary repairs or maintenance issues. Report problems as soon as they arise to ensure a safe and functional living environment. Timely reporting can also help you build a positive relationship with your landlord.

Sharing Responsibilities with Roommates

Establish Clear Expectations: Effective communication is key when sharing living spaces with roommates. Have open discussions about expectations regarding cleanliness, shared expenses, and how responsibilities will be divided. Clarity from the beginning helps prevent misunderstandings and conflicts down the road.

Create a Chore Chart: To ensure fairness and transparency in household chores, consider developing a chore chart that clearly outlines each person's responsibilities. Rotate tasks regularly so that no one feels burdened, and everyone contributes equally to maintaining a clean and organized living space.

Hold Regular Meetings: Maintaining a harmonious living environment with roommates requires ongoing communication. Schedule periodic roommate meetings to discuss any concerns, adjustments to responsibilities, or changes in the living situation. These meetings provide a platform for addressing issues promptly and collaboratively.

Respect Each Other's Space: While shared living spaces come with their benefits, it's important to respect each other's privacy and personal space. Establish guidelines for shared spaces and set boundaries as needed. Mutual respect for one another's space is fundamental to peaceful cohabitation and positive relationships with roommates.

By following these guidelines and fostering open communication, you can effectively manage your household, maintain a clean and organized living space, and cultivate positive relationships with your roommates. This approach ensures a comfortable and enjoyable experience in independent living.

Cooking and Meal Planning

Cooking and meal planning are essential skills for independent living, contributing to a healthier lifestyle and better financial management. This comprehensive guide will help you develop these vital skills, allowing you to create nutritious and diverse meals while staying within your budget. Let's dive deeper into each topic:

Basic Cooking Skills and Techniques

Knife Skills: Mastering fundamental knife skills, such as chopping, dicing, and mincing, not only improves your efficiency in the kitchen but also ensures your safety as you handle sharp utensils.

Cooking Methods: Familiarize yourself with various cooking methods like sautéing, roasting, boiling, steaming, and baking. Each method offers unique flavors and textures to your dishes, adding variety to your meals.

Temperature Control: Understand the significance of temperature control, especially when cooking proteins. Using a food thermometer to ensure meats reach the recommended internal temperature for safe consumption is crucial for your well-being.

Seasoning and Flavoring: Experiment with herbs, spices, and flavorings to elevate the taste of your dishes. Learning how to balance flavors and use seasonings effectively will allow you to create delicious meals with your unique touch.

Grocery Shopping on a Budget

Create a Shopping List: Plan your weekly meals and create a shopping list based on the necessary ingredients. Sticking to your list will help you avoid impulsive and unplanned purchases, saving you money in the long run.

Buy in Bulk: Consider buying non-perishable items like rice, pasta, and canned goods in bulk. This cost-effective approach can significantly reduce your grocery expenses over time.

Explore Generic Brands: Don't hesitate to try generic or store-brand products. They are often more budget-friendly than name brands while maintaining good quality.

Shop Seasonally: Opt for seasonal fruits and vegetables, as they are usually more abundant and affordable. Embracing seasonal produce not only helps you save money but also adds variety to your diet.

Meal Planning for a Healthy Diet

Balanced Meals: Aim for balanced meals that incorporate proteins, carbohydrates, healthy fats, and a generous portion of fruits and vegetables. A well-rounded diet promotes overall health and well-being.

Portion Control: Practice portion control to prevent overeating. Using smaller plates and bowls can naturally regulate your portion sizes and assist in maintaining a healthy weight.

Meal Prepping: Embrace meal prepping by preparing ingredients in advance or cooking meals for the week. This time-saving technique ensures you have healthy options readily available and reduces the temptation to order takeout on busy days.

Diverse Protein Sources: Incorporate a variety of protein sources into your diet, such as lean meats, poultry, fish, beans, legumes, and plant-based alternatives. Diverse protein choices provide essential nutrients and keep your meals interesting.

Preparing Meals at Home

Plan Weekly Menus: Organize your weekly menus while considering your schedule and available cooking time. This approach streamlines your grocery shopping and meal preparation processes, making your life easier.

Batch Cooking: Consider batch cooking and storing leftovers for future meals. This efficient method saves you time and reduces the need for daily cooking, allowing you to enjoy a home-cooked meal even on busy days.

Explore New Recipes: Keep your meals exciting and diverse by experimenting with new recipes. Explore the vast array of options available online and in cookbooks to discover new flavors and cooking techniques.

Mindful Eating: Cultivate mindful eating habits by savoring your meals without distractions. This practice promotes a healthier relationship with food, enhances your appreciation for flavors, and can aid in weight management.

With these insights and practical tips, you'll be well-equipped to develop your cooking skills, shop smartly on a budget, and maintain a nutritious and satisfying diet at home, all while expanding your culinary horizons. Happy cooking!

Car Insurance

Car insurance is an indispensable component of responsible car ownership that offers vital financial protection in case of accidents or damage to your vehicle. Understanding car insurance is essential for young adults, as it provides security and is mandated by law in many states. In this guide, we'll delve deeper into the importance of car insurance, its various types, and how to select coverage that suits your needs and budget.

Why Car Insurance Matters

Car insurance is much more than a legal requirement; it's a financial safeguard and a source of peace of mind.

Financial Safeguard: Car insurance acts as a financial safety net, shielding you from bearing the full financial burden of unexpected accidents or vehicle-related damages. Without insurance, these costs could be overwhelming and disrupt your financial stability.

Legal Requirement: In numerous states, having a minimum car insurance coverage is a legal requirement. Failing to meet these requirements can result in fines, license suspension, or legal consequences. It's essential to comply with your state's laws to avoid these consequences.

Peace of Mind: Car insurance offers peace of mind while driving. Knowing that you have coverage in place can alleviate stress and anxiety associated with the uncertainties of the road. This peace of mind allows you to focus on driving safely.

Understanding Types of Car Insurance Coverage

Car insurance consists of several types of coverage, each serving a specific purpose. When choosing coverage, ask questions to your insurance agency to understand which types are best for you:

Liability Coverage: This coverage pays for bodily injury and property damage to others in an accident where you are at fault. It is typically required by law. Ask about the minimum liability coverage your state mandates.

Collision Coverage: Collision coverage compensates for damage to your vehicle resulting from a collision, regardless of fault. Consider whether this coverage is necessary based on your vehicle's value and how prone you are to accidents.

Comprehensive Coverage: Comprehensive coverage covers non-collision-related damages, such as theft, vandalism, or natural disasters. It's essential to understand the deductibles and limits associated with comprehensive coverage.

Uninsured/Underinsured Motorist Coverage: This coverage protects you if you are involved in an accident with a driver with insufficient or no insurance. Ask about the coverage limits and whether it includes protection against hit-and-run accidents.

Medical Payments Coverage: Medical payment coverage helps pay for medical expenses incurred due to an accident, regardless of fault. Inquire about coverage limits and whether it includes passengers in your vehicle.

Personal Injury Protection (PIP): PIP covers medical expenses, lost wages, and other related costs for you and your passengers after an accident, regardless of fault. Ask about the scope of coverage and any additional benefits.

Selecting the Right Coverage

When choosing car insurance, assessing your needs and financial situation is crucial. Ask the following questions to determine the right coverage for you:

State Requirements: Understand your state's minimum insurance requirements, as they vary from state to state. Make sure you meet these requirements while considering additional coverage.

Budget: Determine how much you can comfortably spend on car insurance premiums while meeting your other financial obligations. Don't forget to ask about available discounts.

Vehicle Value: Consider the value of your vehicle. Older vehicles may not require as much coverage as new or high-value ones. Ask about the coverage options for different vehicle types.

Driving Habits: Evaluate your driving habits, such as daily commute distance, where you park your car, and the likelihood of accidents in your area. Ask about coverage options that suit your specific driving circumstances.

Additional Coverage: Assess whether additional coverages, like comprehensive or collision, are necessary based on your vehicle's value and the potential risks you face. Ask about the cost-benefit analysis of these coverages.

Deductibles: Choose deductibles that align with your budget and risk tolerance. A higher deductible typically results in lower premiums. Still, you'll pay more out of pocket in the event of a claim. Ask about deductible options and their impact on premiums.

In summary, car insurance is a legal requirement in many states and a critical financial safeguard. It's essential to understand the various types of coverage and ask questions to your insurance agency to select a plan tailored to your needs and budget. By doing so, you'll drive confidently, knowing you're protected in case of unexpected events.

Safety and Emergency Preparedness

Ensuring safety and being prepared for emergencies are paramount, especially for young adults transitioning to independent living. This comprehensive guide covers fire safety, emergency kits, evacuation plans, and staying safe during severe weather, with a focus on organization, clarity, and providing context to help you navigate potential challenges effectively:

Fire Safety and Prevention

Smoke Alarms: Your first line of defense against fires is a working smoke alarm. Install smoke alarms in critical areas of your residence, including bedrooms and common areas. Test them regularly and replace batteries as needed to ensure they function correctly. Smoke alarms are your early warning system in case of a fire.

Escape Routes: Take the time to familiarize yourself with your home's layout and identify multiple escape routes. Plan and practice evacuation drills, particularly if you share your living space with roommates. Having a clear escape plan is vital in high-stress situations.

Fire Extinguishers: Ensuring your safety and the safety of those around you is paramount. Have a fire safety plan in place, complete with designated meeting points and escape routes. Keep a fire extinguisher or fire blanket in an easily accessible location, and make sure you understand how to use it. Regularly check the extinguisher's expiration date to ensure it remains effective. Knowing how to operate these life-saving tools can make a significant difference during a small fire incident, providing you with peace of mind and the ability to respond swiftly and effectively if the need arises. Everyone in the house should know where the tools are and how to use them.

Cooking Safety: Practice safe cooking habits, such as staying in the kitchen while cooking, keeping flammable items away from heat sources, and turning off appliances when not in use. Cooking-related fires are among the most common residential fires, and prevention is key. This is where having a fire safety blanket nearby can save you and your home.

Creating an Emergency Kit

Vehicle Emergency Kit: When assembling your vehicle emergency kit, consider including solar-powered or hand-cranked tools that don't rely on batteries. These eco-friendly options can be invaluable in emergencies. If you live in an area prone to snowy conditions, don't forget to add a bag of kitty litter to your kit. It can provide traction if your vehicle gets stuck in snow or ice, helping you get back on the road safely. Your preparedness and resourcefulness will be your greatest allies during unexpected situations on the road.

Personal Needs: Tailor your emergency kit to your specific needs, including any required medications, hygiene products, and comfort items. Consider the unique needs of all household members, including pets.

Emergency Contacts: Include a list of emergency contacts in your kit, such as family members, friends, and local authorities, for quick reference during crises. Ensure everyone in your household knows how to use these contacts.

Regular Refresh: Periodically check and refresh your emergency kit, ensuring all items are in good condition and that food and water supplies have not expired. Make it a habit to review your kit at least once a year.

Evacuation Plans and Drills

Establish Meeting Points: Define specific meeting points outside your residence for evacuation. This ensures that everyone can be accounted for in case of an emergency. Share these meeting points with all household members.

Practice Evacuation Drills: Conduct regular evacuation drills, especially when sharing living space with others. Practice using various exit routes to enhance preparedness. Familiarity with evacuation routes reduces panic during emergencies.

Communication Plan: Develop a communication plan with roommates or neighbors to effectively relay vital information during an evacuation or emergency. Ensure that everyone knows how to contact each other in case of separation.

Know Community Resources: Familiarize yourself with local community resources, including emergency shelters and evacuation centers. This knowledge is essential if temporary relocation becomes necessary. Research and have a list of nearby emergency facilities.

Staying Safe in Severe Weather

Weather Alerts: Stay informed about weather conditions by utilizing weather apps, following local news, and subscribing to emergency alerts, ensuring you receive timely information. Being aware of changing weather patterns is crucial for proactive safety measures.

Emergency Weather Plans: Develop comprehensive plans

for severe weather scenarios, such as storms, hurricanes, or tornadoes. Know where to take shelter and designate safe areas within your home. Create a "safe room" if needed.

Emergency Communication: Ensure that your phone remains charged and has alternative communication methods, such as a battery-powered radio, in case of power outages that disrupt regular communication channels. Reliable communication is vital during severe weather.

Emergency Contacts: Share emergency contacts with roommates or neighbors and establish a system for checking in on each other during severe weather events to enhance community safety. Working together can provide mutual support and assistance.

By prioritizing fire safety, creating a well-equipped emergency kit, practicing evacuation plans, and staying informed about severe weather, you can enhance your safety and that of others in your living space. These proactive measures empower you to respond effectively in emergencies, fostering a secure and prepared living environment. Remember, preparedness and knowledge are your best allies in times of crisis.

Key Takeaways

Financial Preparedness for Independent Living

- Assess your finances thoroughly, including income and expenses.

- Consider not only rent but also additional costs like utilities and groceries.
- Follow the 30% rule, spending no more than 30% of your income on rent.

Choosing the Right Location

- Select a location convenient for work or school to minimize commuting time and costs.
- Prioritize neighborhood safety and proximity to essential services and amenities.
- Consider your lifestyle preferences, such as urban or suburban living.

Apartment Hunting Tips

- Start your search early to have ample time for research.
- Utilize online platforms and attend open houses to find the right apartment.
- Create a checklist of essential features and ask the landlord questions.

Understanding Lease Agreements

- Carefully read and understand the lease agreement, including rent, duration, and maintenance clauses.
- Seek clarification on any ambiguous terms and understand security deposit details.

- Document the property's condition before moving in to protect your security deposit.

Ongoing Skills for Independent Living

- Independent living is an ongoing journey that involves managing your household, maintaining a clean living space, and fostering positive relationships with roommates.
- Regular decluttering, creating cleaning schedules, and sharing responsibilities with roommates are key to an organized and harmonious living environment.
- Basic home repair skills, emergency preparedness, and roommate communication contribute to a successful independent living experience.

Test Your Knowledge

1. When budgeting for rent, it's recommended not to spend more than what percentage of your monthly income?

- a. 40%
- b. 50%
- c. 30%
- d. 20%

2. What should you consider when choosing an apartment location?

- a. Proximity to shopping malls
- b. Proximity to work or school
- c. Noise level in the area
- d. Number of parks nearby

3. Before signing a lease agreement, it's essential to carefully read and understand all the _____ to avoid any surprises later.

4. Regular decluttering and creating a cleaning schedule helps in maintaining a _____ living space.

5. True or False: Emergency preparedness includes having a well-equipped emergency kit with essentials like non-perishable food and water.

6 TECHNOLOGY AND ONLINE LIFE

I n the digital age, our lives have become increasingly intertwined with the online world. From socializing and shopping to studying and working, the internet plays a central role in our daily activities. While this connectivity offers incredible opportunities and convenience, it also brings about potential risks and challenges. This chapter is dedicated to helping you navigate the digital landscape safely and responsibly. We'll explore the importance of online security, responsible social media use, the significance of online privacy, and how to stay safe when engaging in online transactions. To drive home the significance of these topics, let's delve into the cautionary tale of Sean, a young individual who learned the hard way about the perils of neglecting online safety.

Sean's Cautionary Tale:

Meet Sean, a friendly and outgoing guy who loved exploring the online world. Sean had a diverse group of online friends, one of whom he had known for months through social media. They chatted regularly, sharing stories and experiences as if they'd known each other for years.

One day, Sean received a message from one of his friends on Snapchat, who claimed to be in a tight spot. They said they were stranded without gas money and needed help urgently. Trusting his friend, Sean didn't hesitate to offer assistance. He transferred the money without a second thought, thinking he was helping out a friend in need.

As the days passed, Sean realized he had fallen victim to a scam. He discovered that his friend's account had been hacked, and the person he had been helping was not his friend at all. This unfortunate experience left Sean feeling vulnerable and betrayed. He was thankful it was only $50 as it could have been much worse but it was a harsh lesson on the importance of online security and responsible online interactions. Through Sean's story, we'll explore how learning to protect yourself online can prevent similar hardships and ensure a safer and more enjoyable digital experience.

Digital Literacy and Online Security

Understanding Digital Literacy: In today's digital age, developing digital literacy means more than knowing how to use a computer; it's about navigating the complex online world with wisdom. It involves recognizing different file types, understanding common software applications, and honing critical thinking skills. Think of it as learning the rules of a vast digital game where critical thinking is your best strategy against misinformation.

Internet Safety: As you explore the online world, your safety should be a top concern. From recognizing malicious websites to understanding concepts like cookies and tracking, internet safety practices are like your shield against digital dangers. Knowing how to use secure Wi-Fi connections is akin to locking your virtual doors. Public Wi-Fi networks can be risky, just like leaving your front door wide open.

Media Literacy: In today's digital media era, being media literate is like having a pair of glasses that help you see through biases in news and content. It's also about distinguishing between credible and unreliable sources, like having a truth detector. Developing media literacy skills empowers you to navigate the vast online landscape with discernment.

Protecting Your Personal Information Online: Safeguarding your online presence is like safeguarding a treasure chest. Learning how to adjust privacy settings on social media platforms is your way of controlling who gets a glimpse of your treasures. Minimal sharing is a practice akin to not displaying all your treasures in public; avoid oversharing sensitive details like your address, phone number, or financial info. Using secure Wi-Fi connections is like sending your treasure chest via a secure courier. Being skeptical of requests for personal information is your shield against treasure hunters.

Recognizing Online Scams and Phishing: Familiarizing yourself with common phishing techniques is like learning to spot traps in an adventure game. Verifying the legitimacy of emails and ensuring the security of websites you interact with are skills that protect you from falling into digital traps.

Password Best Practices: Think of passwords as keys to your digital castle. Creating complex and unique passwords is akin to having intricate locks on each door. Regularly changing passwords is like changing locks regularly. It's an extra layer of security to keep your castle safe.

Two-Factor Authentication

Enable Two-Factor Authentication (2FA): Two-Factor Authentication (2FA) is like having an extra lock on your treasure chest. It requires a second form of verification beyond your password, like a secret handshake. Enabling 2FA adds a critical layer of security to your online accounts.

Authentication Apps: While using text messages for 2FA is more secure than not having it at all, authentication apps take your security up a notch. They're like enchanted keys that work offline and can't be easily swiped by digital thieves.

Secure Backup: Think of backup codes as spare keys to your treasure chest. Safely storing these codes is crucial in case you lose your primary way of accessing your accounts.

Device Trustworthiness: Trustworthy devices are like trusted companions on your digital journey. Use them for secure access to your accounts, just like you'd trust a loyal friend. Avoid logging into sensitive accounts on untrusted devices to minimize the risk of unauthorized access.

Social Media Use and Online Etiquette

Responsible Social Media Posting: Think of your social media posts as messages in bottles. Consider the potential consequences before posting; once it's out there, it's hard to erase. Respecting others' privacy is essential for building and maintaining trust online. Promoting positivity is like being a beacon of light in a sea of negativity.

Interacting with Others on Social Media: Engage with empathy and active listening. It's like understanding different characters in a digital story. Handling online disagreements maturely with credible sources and facts helps maintain productive dialogue.

Online Reputation Management: Think of your online reputation as your digital resume. Regularly curate your digital presence to reflect your growth and maturity. Consider how potential employers or colleagues might perceive your online image. Positive contributions to online communities, like sharing valuable content and engaging in meaningful discussions, make a difference in others' lives.

By adopting these practices, you'll navigate the digital land-scape wisely and protect your online privacy and security effectively.

Purchasing and Meeting Online

For college-aged young adults venturing into online transactions, comprehending the intricacies of online shopping, arranging meetings with sellers or buyers, ensuring secure transactions, and adhering to online marketplace etiquette is paramount. Here is an extensive guide to help you navigate these aspects:

Online Shopping and Transaction Safety

Prioritize Secure Websites: Make secure websites with "https://" in the URL your first choice for online shopping. Stick to well-established online retailers known for their history of secure transactions.

Choose Trusted Platforms: Rely on trusted online shopping platforms. Platforms equipped with buyer protection mechanisms offer an additional layer of transaction security.

Opt for Secure Payment Methods: Select secure methods like credit cards or payment gateways with robust security features when making payments. Avoid transmitting sensitive information through unsecured channels.

Review Seller Ratings: Inspect seller reviews and ratings before making a purchase. Insights from previous buyers can help gauge the seller's reliability.

Ensuring Secure Transactions

Verify Product Details: Before completing a transaction, verify product details such as specifications, condition, and authenticity. Effective communication with the seller or buyer is essential.

Consider Escrow Services: For high-value transactions, contemplate using escrow services. These services hold funds until both parties fulfill their obligations, ensuring a secure transaction process.

Monitor Shipments: When purchasing items online, monitor the shipment's progress using the provided tracking numbers. Staying informed about the delivery status ensures a smooth process.

Understand Return Policies: Familiarize yourself with the return policies of online sellers. Understanding the return process can be crucial if the received item exceeds expectations.

Online Marketplace Etiquette

Maintain Clear Communication: Uphold clear and respectful communication with sellers or buyers. Address any queries or concerns before finalizing a transaction.

Timely Responses: Respond promptly to messages or inquiries. Timely communication fosters a positive buying or selling experience.

Provide Honest Descriptions: When selling items, furnish honest and accurate descriptions. Transparency builds trust between buyers and sellers.

Leave Feedback: After concluding a transaction, take a moment to leave feedback for the seller or buyer. Positive feedback acknowledges a smooth transaction, while constructive feedback can aid others in making informed decisions.

Meeting Sellers or Buyers in Person

If you're planning to meet someone whose ad you responded to in person, taking precautions is crucial to ensure your safety and a successful transaction. Here are some valuable tips:

Select Safe Meeting Spots

Public and Well-Lit Locations: Choose meeting places that are public, well-lit, and populated. Opt for venues with surveillance cameras and a steady flow of people. Consider places like shopping mall parking lots, coffee shops, or local police stations as meeting spots.

Daylight Hours: Whenever possible, schedule meetings during daylight hours. Daytime meetings offer better visibility and reduce potential risks associated with meeting at night.

Bring a Companion

Bringing a Friend: Whenever feasible, bring a friend or family member with you to the meeting. Having another person present provides an additional layer of security and can deter potential scammers or dishonest individuals.

Inform a Trusted Contact

Notify Someone: Before the meeting, inform a trusted friend or family member about your plans. Share essential details such as the meeting location, time, and the identity of the person you'll be meeting. Let them know when you expect to return.

Check-In: Arrange a check-in time with your trusted contact. After the meeting, contact them to confirm your safety and the successful completion of the transaction.

Trust Your Intuition

Listen to Your Gut: Trust your instincts during the meeting. If something doesn't feel right or seems uncomfortable, don't hesitate to take action. Your safety should always be the top priority.

Cancel or Relocate: If you have any doubts about the meeting or the other person's intentions, consider canceling the meeting or relocating it to a more public and secure setting. Your well-being is paramount.

Inspect Before Paying

Inspect the Product: Before making any payment, thoroughly inspect the product you intend to purchase. Ensure it meets your expectations and matches the description provided in the ad. Don't rush this process; take your time to examine the item carefully.

Payment Caution: Never pay for the product in advance or send money electronically without first inspecting the item in person. Scammers may ask for payment upfront and disappear once they receive the funds.

By following these guidelines when meeting sellers or buyers in person, you can minimize risks, protect your safety, and increase the likelihood of a successful and secure transaction. Remember that being cautious and prioritizing your well-being is essential when conducting in-person transactions with individuals you've met online.

You can securely navigate the digital marketplace by adhering to these guidelines for online shopping and transactions, arranging meetings with sellers or buyers, ensuring secure transactions, and practicing online marketplace etiquette. These practices contribute to a positive online commerce experience while minimizing potential risks.

Key Takeaways

Prioritize Online Security: Developing digital literacy and safeguarding personal information is crucial in the digital age. Take steps to protect your online presence, including setting strong passwords, enabling two-factor authentication, and being cautious about sharing personal information.

Practice Responsible Social Media Use: Social media plays a significant role in your online life. Think before you post, respect others' privacy, and engage in positive and constructive interactions. Your online reputation matters and can impact your personal and professional life.

Understand the Importance of Online Privacy: Your online privacy is essential for personal security. Be mindful of what you share online, adjust privacy settings on social media platforms, and practice secure browsing to minimize tracking and potential threats.

Stay Safe in Online Transactions: Whether you're shopping online or meeting someone for a transaction, prioritize safety. Choose secure websites, verify product details, and meet in well-lit, public locations when necessary. Responsible online marketplace etiquette can enhance your online commerce experience.

Continuously Educate Yourself: The digital landscape is constantly evolving. Stay informed about online privacy issues, emerging threats, and best practices. By staying educated, you empower yourself to navigate the digital world safely and responsibly.

Test Your Knowledge

1. What does HTTPS in a website URL indicate?

- a. High-speed Internet connection
- b. Highly Secure Encryption Protocol

- d. Hyperlinked Text and Secure Pages
- c. High-Efficiency Transaction Service

2. Which of the following is NOT a recommended practice for online privacy?

- a. Using a Virtual Private Network (VPN)
- b. Regularly reviewing and customizing privacy settings on social media.
- c. Conducting sensitive transactions on public Wi-Fi networks
- d. Adjusting browser privacy settings to minimize tracking

3. What is the purpose of Two-Factor Authentication (2FA)?

- a. It requires two separate internet connections for added security.
- b. It verifies your identity with a fingerprint and a passcode.
- c. It adds an extra layer of security by requiring a second form of verification.
- d. It encrypts all your online communications.

4. When meeting sellers or buyers in person for transactions, it's important to choose _____, well-lit, and public locations.

5. Leaving constructive feedback after an online transaction can help others make informed decisions. (True/False)

7 MENTAL HEALTH AND WELL-BEING

Picture this: Boston, a young adult with a zest for life, decided to take the plunge and move to a new city in pursuit of an exciting job opportunity. Leaving behind the comfort of home, old friends, and the ever-supportive embrace of family, Boston was ready to embrace independence and kickstart a new chapter.

But as the initial thrill of adventure settled, the reality of being on his own started to sink in. Friends were miles away, and adulting came with a whole bunch of responsibilities he hadn't quite prepared for. What was once a thrilling escapade quickly turned into a battle against feelings of isolation and overwhelm, threatening to overshadow his journey.

And then, there was work. Boston's newfound struggles weren't going unnoticed. A perceptive colleague named

Michael spotted the change in him. Instead of brushing it off, Michael decided to lend a helping hand. It might have seemed like a small gesture, but it made a world of difference.

Through heartfelt conversations and shared experiences, Boston learned the power of opening up about his struggles. He discovered that it's okay to ask for help and that vulnerability can be a strength. With the support of friends like Alex, Boston not only salvaged his job but embarked on a journey of self-discovery and emotional growth.

Now, as we dive into this chapter, we're entering the world of mental health and well-being, a place where stories like Boston's are part of the journey. Here, we'll explore the fundamental principles that underlie your emotional and mental health during this transformative phase of life.

This chapter will equip you with the tools to protect your mental well-being, help you recognize when it's time to seek assistance, and lay the groundwork for emotional resilience. We'll delve into strategies for personal growth, nurturing positive relationships, and providing you with the resources needed to navigate the complexities of young adulthood.

Your mental well-being is like a compass, guiding you through uncharted waters and helping you carve a path to lasting success and a life filled with fulfillment. Welcome to the world of mental health and well-being, where you hold the pen to craft your own story of growth and resilience.

What Is Mental Health?

It's not just a fancy term; it's all about how you're doing on the inside – emotionally, mentally, and socially. Think of it as the backstage pass to your life, influencing how you handle stress, connect with others, and make those everyday decisions. But here's the deal: it's not just about dodging mental disorders; it's about rocking life's ups and downs, building awesome relationships, and staying on top of your game.

The Importance of Mental Health

Holistic Well-Being: Holistic well-being emphasizes the interconnectedness of various aspects of your health. Mental health is a fundamental pillar in this framework, as it closely interacts with physical health and emotional stability. When nurtured, it contributes to an integrated sense of wellness that harmonizes these elements, fostering a balanced and healthy state of being.

Quality of Life: The influence of mental health on your quality of life cannot be overstated. A well-maintained mental state enriches your existence with a profound sense of purpose, satisfaction, and the capacity to derive meaning from every facet of life, both mundane and exceptional.

Coping with Stress: Mental well-being equips you with an array of effective stress-coping mechanisms. These tools enhance your capacity to withstand and adapt to life's inevitable challenges. By promoting resilience and adaptability, good mental health fortifies you against the adverse effects of stress.

Productivity and Success: Mental health is an invaluable asset on your journey to academic and professional success. It plays a pivotal role in sharpening cognitive faculties, enhancing decision-making abilities, and propelling you toward your personal and career goals. A well-maintained mental state provides the clarity and determination needed to achieve success.

Interpersonal Relationships: The impact of mental health extends to your interpersonal relationships. It molds your ability to communicate effectively, empathize with others, and cultivate meaningful connections. A strong foundation in mental health can greatly enhance the quality and depth of your relationships.

Emotional Regulation: Proficiency in emotional regulation is a core aspect of mental health. It empowers you to comprehend and manage your emotions in a constructive and adaptive manner. This skill ensures that you can navigate the spectrum of human feelings while maintaining emotional equilibrium.

Reducing Stigma: Prioritizing mental health initiatives is instrumental in combating the persistent stigma surrounding mental health issues. Initiating open and honest dialogues, coupled with widespread awareness campaigns, plays a pivotal role in fostering a more compassionate and understanding society. By reducing stigma, we pave the way for individuals to seek and receive the support they need without fear or discrimination.

Common Mental Health Challenges

Anxiety Disorders: Anxiety disorders indeed encompass various types, as mentioned earlier. In addition to generalized anxiety disorder, panic disorder, and social anxiety disorder, it's worth noting other types such as specific phobias (intense fears of specific objects or situations) and obsessive-compulsive disorder (characterized by persistent, intrusive thoughts and repetitive behaviors).

Depression: Depression is indeed a significant mood disorder. It's essential to emphasize that there are different forms of depression, including major depressive disorder (characterized by persistent sadness and a loss of interest or pleasure in activities), seasonal affective disorder (depression that occurs at specific times of the year, often in the winter), and persistent depressive disorder (a long-lasting form of depression).

Stress-Related Disorders: Chronic stress can indeed lead to various physical and mental health challenges. It's important to mention that stress-related disorders can also include adjustment disorders (excessive stress or difficulty coping with significant life changes), acute stress disorder (resulting from exposure to a traumatic event), and complex PTSD (a more severe form of PTSD often stemming from prolonged trauma or multiple traumatic events).

Eating Disorders: In addition to anorexia nervosa, bulimia nervosa, and binge-eating disorder, there are other eating disorders to be aware of, such as avoidant/restrictive food

intake disorder (ARFID), which involves limited food preferences and aversions, and orthorexia nervosa, characterized
by an obsession with healthy eating.

Substance Use Disorders: Alongside substance abuse, it's
essential to mention substance dependence, which involves
physical and psychological reliance on a substance, as well as
co-occurring disorders (individuals who experience both a
mental health disorder and a substance use disorder simultaneously).

Attention-Deficit/Hyperactivity Disorder (ADHD): In addition to academic and occupational performance, ADHD can
also impact relationships and daily functioning. It's valuable
to know that there are three types of ADHD: primarily inat-
tentive presentation (predominantly difficulties with attention), primarily hyperactive-impulsive presentation
(predominantly hyperactivity and impulsivity), and
combined presentation (a mix of inattention, hyperactivity,
and impulsivity).

Bipolar Disorder: Bipolar disorder is characterized by
extreme mood swings, including manic episodes (elevated
mood, increased energy, and impulsivity) and depressive
episodes (profound sadness and loss of interest). Understanding the nuances of this disorder can help individuals
manage it effectively.

Schizophrenia: Schizophrenia is a severe mental disorder
that affects thinking, emotions, and behavior. Symptoms

may include hallucinations, delusions, disorganized thinking, and impaired social functioning.

Recognizing Mental Health Warning Signs

Changes in Behavior: Be alert to noticeable shifts in behavior, such as increasing isolation, withdrawing from social activities, or showing a sudden decline in interests and hobbies. These changes may indicate underlying mental health concerns.

Mood Swings: Extreme mood swings, persistent feelings of sadness, irritability, or heightened anxiety that significantly impact daily functioning should be noted. These mood fluctuations may suggest the need for mental health support.

Sleep Disturbances: Pay attention to significant changes in sleep patterns, including persistent insomnia or excessive sleeping. Sleep disruptions can often be early indicators of emotional distress.

Appetite Changes: Noticeable shifts in appetite leading to significant weight loss or gain should be observed. Changes in eating habits can be linked to emotional well-being.

Energy Levels: Persistent fatigue, low energy levels, or a lack of motivation that hinders regular activities can be indicative of underlying mental health challenges.

Cognitive Challenges: Be aware of difficulties in concentration, decision-making, or experiencing memory lapses. Cognitive challenges may signal emotional distress and should not be overlooked.

Physical Symptoms: Unexplained physical symptoms like frequent headaches, stomachaches, or unexplained bodily pains should be taken seriously, as they can be linked to mental health issues.

Self-Harm or Risky Behavior: Be vigilant about signs of self-harming behaviors or engaging in risky activities without consideration for consequences. These actions may be expressions of emotional turmoil.

Identifying Signs of Mental Health Struggles

Social Withdrawal: Recognize when individuals avoid social interactions, isolate themselves from friends, family, or regular activities. Social withdrawal can be a red flag for mental health struggles.

Expressing Hopelessness: Pay attention when someone verbalizes feelings of hopelessness, worthlessness, or expresses a belief that life is not worth living. These expressions may indicate severe emotional distress.

Changes in Academic Performance: Be attuned to significant declines in academic performance or signs of disengagement from educational pursuits. Academic changes can often reflect underlying mental health challenges.

Substance Use: Notice any escalation in substance use as a coping mechanism for mental health struggles. Self-medication through substances can indicate underlying emotional difficulties.

Increased Anxiety: Acknowledge heightened anxiety levels, panic attacks, or an inability to manage stress. Increased anxiety may be a sign that someone is struggling emotionally.

Neglecting Self-Care: Observe when individuals neglect personal hygiene, appearance, or self-care routines. Lack of self-care can be linked to mental health issues.

Lack of Interest: Take note when someone loses interest in activities they once enjoyed or displays a decreased passion for their hobbies. A decline in enthusiasm may indicate emotional challenges.

How to Approach Someone in Need

Express Concern: Approach the person with empathy, expressing genuine concern for their well-being. Let them know you care and are there to support them.

Listen Actively: Provide a non-judgmental and compassionate space for them to express their feelings. Active listening is crucial for creating a safe environment.

Ask Direct Questions: If appropriate, ask direct but caring questions about their mental health. For example, say, "I've noticed some changes; how are you feeling?" This shows you're open to discussing their emotions.

Offer Assistance: Extend your support and assistance in seeking professional help through counseling services, therapy, or mental health resources. Be proactive in helping them access the necessary support.

Encourage Professional Help: Encourage them to reach out to mental health professionals for guidance and support. Highlight the importance of seeking expert assistance when facing emotional difficulties.

Reducing Mental Health Stigma

Education and Awareness: Promote education and awareness about mental health to dispel myths and misconceptions. Understanding mental health is a crucial step in reducing stigma.

Open Conversations: Foster open conversations about mental health, creating a supportive environment where individuals feel comfortable sharing their experiences and seeking help when needed.

Share Personal Stories: Share personal stories of overcoming mental health challenges to inspire hope and reduce stigma. Sharing experiences can help others feel less alone in their struggles.

Language Matters: Be mindful of the language used when discussing mental health. Use respectful, inclusive, and non-stigmatizing language that fosters understanding and compassion.

Supportive Communities: Work towards building supportive communities where individuals feel safe seeking help without fear of judgment. Community support is essential for breaking down stigma barriers.

By recognizing these mental health warning signs, identifying signs of mental health struggles, approaching individuals with care and support, and actively working to reduce mental health stigma, we can collectively contribute to a culture of empathy, understanding, and unwavering support. Creating an environment where mental health is openly discussed and prioritized is instrumental in building resilient and compassionate communities.

Effective Coping Mechanisms

Mindfulness Meditation: Embrace mindfulness meditation to stay present and nurture a non-judgmental awareness of your thoughts and emotions. Meditation isn't just about relaxation; it's about enhancing focus and taming stress. Consider using mindfulness apps or guided meditation sessions to get started.

Deep Breathing Exercises: Incorporate deep breathing exercises into your daily routine to tackle stress and anxiety head-on. Controlled breathing acts as a calming agent, contributing to your overall well-being. You can find various breathing techniques online or through mobile apps.

Physical Activity: Regular physical activity is your ally in this journey. Exercise releases endorphins, your body's natural mood elevators, promoting physical and mental health. Find an activity you enjoy, whether it's jogging, dancing, or yoga, and make it a part of your routine.

Journaling: Grab a journal and pour your thoughts and feelings into it. Writing can be therapeutic, helping you process emotions, gain clarity, and sometimes discover new facets of yourself. Consider daily journaling prompts to kickstart your writing practice.

Social Connections: Nurture your social connections. Spending quality time with friends and loved ones provides emotional support and a profound sense of belonging. Reach out to friends for regular catch-ups, and make an effort to strengthen your social bonds.

Positive Affirmations: Empower yourself with positive affirmations. These little mantras can challenge and reshape negative self-talk, boosting self-esteem and fostering a positive mindset. Create a list of affirmations that resonate with you and recite them daily.

Artistic Expression: Dive into creative outlets like art, music, or writing. Expressing yourself creatively can be a powerful way to navigate the turbulent sea of emotions. You don't need to be a professional artist; the act of creating itself can be therapeutic.

The Role of Self-Care

Prioritize Rest: Give yourself the gift of sufficient sleep. Quality sleep is a cornerstone of cognitive function, mood regulation, and well-being. Establish a consistent sleep schedule and create a bedtime routine that promotes relaxation.

Healthy Nutrition: What you eat directly affects your physical and mental health. Opt for a balanced and nutritious diet to fuel your journey to well-being. Include a variety of fruits, vegetables, lean proteins, and whole grains in your meals.

Establish Boundaries: Learn to set and maintain healthy boundaries in your relationships and work. These boundaries are not just limits but shields guarding your well-being. Communicate your boundaries clearly to those around you.

Time Management: Master the art of time management. Prioritize tasks, set achievable goals, and ensure you allocate time for both work and leisure. Consider using time management techniques like the Pomodoro Technique or task prioritization methods.

Digital Detox: Unplug from screens periodically. Constant digital exposure can contribute to stress and impact your mental health. Give yourself the gift of a digital detox by designating tech-free hours or days to recharge.

Pamper Yourself: Make self-pampering a ritual. Whether indulging in a relaxing bath, losing yourself in a favorite hobby, or taking a leisurely walk, prioritize activities that bring you joy. Schedule regular "me-time" to recharge your spirit.

Learn to Say No: Practice the art of saying no when necessary. Overcommitting can lead to burnout. Prioritize your well-being by managing your commitments wisely. Remember that saying no to one thing often means saying yes to yourself.

Developing Your Self-Care Routine

Self-Reflection: Reflect on activities that bring you peace and joy. Identify those who contribute to your well-being, and let them become your daily companions. Consider journaling your self-reflections to track your progress.

Consistency is Key: Establish a routine that incorporates self-care activities. Consistency fosters a habit of making your well-being a top priority. Create a daily or weekly self-care schedule that fits seamlessly into your life.

Experiment with Activities: Venture into various self-care activities. Explore the vast world of possibilities, from reading and nature walks to simple moments of quiet reflection. Keep an open mind and experiment with different practices to discover what resonates with you.

Adjust as Needed: Be adaptable with your self-care routine. Life is a dynamic journey, and your self-care toolkit may need adjustments to accommodate changing circumstances. Regularly assess your needs and tweak your routine accordingly to ensure it continues to serve you well.

Stress Management

Identifying Stress and Effective Strategies

Identify Stressors: Acknowledge the sources of stress in your life. Recognizing stressors is the first step in taming them effectively. Keep a journal to track what triggers your stress, helping you gain insight into recurring patterns.

Time Management Techniques: Use time management techniques to organize tasks and prevent feeling over-whelmed. Divide large tasks into smaller, more manageable steps. Consider using time management tools or apps to help structure your day.

Mind-Body Techniques: Embrace mind-body practices like yoga or tai chi. These activities combine physical movement with mindfulness, fostering relaxation. Attend classes or watch online tutorials to get started.

Seek Support: Contact friends, family, or mental health professionals. Sharing your stressors can provide valuable insights and emotional relief. Reach out to support groups or therapists specializing in stress management.

Set Realistic Expectations: Establish attainable expectations for yourself. Perfectionism can be a silent stressor. Embrace a mindset of progress, not perfection, and set achievable goals for yourself.

Humor and Laughter: Inject humor into your life. Laughter is a natural stress reliever that can elevate your mood, even during challenging times. Watch comedies, read funny books, or spend time with people who make you laugh.

Understanding Stress

What Is Stress?: Stress is your body's built-in response to demands and threats. It gears you up to confront or avoid perceived danger. Stress is a part of life, but chronic or excessive stress can adversely affect your physical and mental health.

The Two Types of Stress:

- **Acute Stress:** This is short-term stress triggered by immediate challenges. It's a normal part of life, often motivating quick action. Examples include preparing for a presentation or dealing with a sudden deadline.
- **Chronic Stress:** This is persistent, long-term stress resulting from ongoing pressure, such as work, finances, or relationships. If left unmanaged, chronic stress can harm your health and well-being.

Daily Stress Management Techniques

Time Management: Prioritize tasks and set realistic goals. Breaking tasks into smaller, manageable steps can reduce feelings of overwhelm. Use techniques like the Eisenhower Matrix to prioritize effectively.

Mindfulness and Deep Breathing: Practice mindfulness exercises and techniques to remain calm and composed when faced with daily stressors. Deep breathing exercises, like the 4-7-8 technique, can help you stay grounded.

Physical Activity: Incorporate regular physical activity into your daily life. Exercise reduces stress and contributes to your overall physical and mental well-being. Find an activity you enjoy, whether it's jogging, dancing, or yoga, and make it a part of your routine.

Healthy Nutrition: Maintain a balanced diet with nourishing foods. Proper nutrition supports your well-being and equips your body to handle stress. Focus on consuming a variety of fruits, vegetables, lean proteins, and whole grains.

Social Connections: Cultivate positive social connections. Spending time with friends and loved ones provides emotional support and reduces feelings of isolation. Plan regular gatherings or virtual meet-ups with loved ones.

Establishing Boundaries: Master setting boundaries in your relationships and work. Understanding your limits and communicating them effectively can prevent unnecessary stress. Learn to say "no" when you need to without feeling guilty.

Mindful Breaks: Take short breaks to engage in joyful or relaxed activities during your day. Even a few minutes of mindful breaks can make a significant difference. Practice mini-meditations or go for a short walk to clear your mind.

Strategies for Long-Term Stress Reduction

Regular Exercise Routine: Develop a consistent exercise routine. Physical activity reduces stress and enhances your overall well-being. Aim for at least 150 minutes of moderate-intensity exercise per week.

Mindfulness Practices: Engage in mindfulness practices such as meditation or yoga. These practices cultivate a calm and focused mind, reducing the impact of chronic stress. Start with guided meditation apps or beginner-friendly yoga classes.

Counseling and Therapy: Consider seeking professional counseling or therapy. Speaking with a mental health professional can provide valuable insights and effective coping strategies. Therapy sessions can be conducted in person or online for convenience.

Time for Hobbies: Dedicate time to activities you enjoy. Hobbies and leisure pursuits offer a healthy escape from daily stressors. Whether it's painting, playing a musical instrument, or gardening, prioritize activities that bring you joy.

Healthy Sleep Patterns: Establish and maintain healthy sleep patterns. Quality sleep is crucial for stress management and your overall well-being. Create a comfortable sleep environment and stick to a consistent sleep schedule.

Stress-Reducing Techniques: Learn and practice progressive muscle relaxation, guided imagery, or biofeedback techniques to enhance stress management skills. These techniques can help you manage stress in real-time.

Positive Lifestyle Changes: Make positive lifestyle changes, such as reducing caffeine intake, quitting smoking, or moderating alcohol consumption. These changes contribute to a healthier stress response and overall well-being.

Problem-Solving Skills: Hone your problem-solving skills. Effective strategies for approaching and resolving challenges can significantly reduce the impact of stressors. Consider reading books or taking courses on problem-solving techniques.

Taking a Holistic Approach to Stress Management

Self-Reflection: Regularly reflect on your stressors and how you respond to them. Understanding your triggers is a pivotal step in effective stress management. Journal your reflections to gain deeper insights.

Seeking Support: Don't hesitate to seek support from friends, family, or support groups. Sharing your feelings and experiences can provide valuable emotional relief. Join online or local support groups to connect with others facing similar challenges.

Flexibility and Adaptability: Cultivate flexibility and adaptability in the face of change. Accept that some stressors are beyond your control, and this acceptance can significantly reduce feelings of helplessness. Practice mindfulness to stay present and adaptable.

Positive Outlook: Foster a positive outlook on life. Cultivate gratitude and focus on aspects of life that bring you joy and fulfillment. Maintain a gratitude journal to regularly remind yourself of the positive aspects of your life.

Seeking Professional Help

When to Consider Professional Help

Persistent Distress: If feelings of distress persist and interfere with your daily life, it may be time to seek professional help. It's essential to recognize that seeking help is a proactive step toward better mental health. Therapists are trained to assist individuals in managing and alleviating distressing emotions.

Impact on Functioning: When emotional struggles start affecting your relationships, work, or academic performance, professional intervention can be beneficial. Mental health professionals can help you develop coping strategies and provide support to regain control over your life.

Changes in Behavior: Significant changes in behavior, such as withdrawal, excessive anger, or risky actions, may indicate the need for professional support. These behavioral changes can be signs of underlying emotional or psychological issues that require attention and guidance.

Intense Emotions: Experiencing intense and overwhelming emotions, such as anxiety or sadness, that are difficult to manage on your own can be a clear signal to seek professional help. Therapists can teach you techniques to regulate your emotions effectively.

Trauma or Loss: Coping with trauma, grief, or significant life changes may necessitate the guidance of a mental health professional. Traumatic experiences and grief can have a profound impact on mental well-being, and therapy can provide a structured and supportive environment for healing.

Substance Use Issues: If substance use becomes problematic and begins to impact various aspects of your life, seeking professional help is crucial. Substance abuse often co-occurs with underlying mental health issues, and addressing both simultaneously is essential for recovery.

How to Find and Choose a Therapist

Referrals: Seek recommendations from friends, family, or primary care providers. Personal referrals often provide valuable insights into the therapist's effectiveness and compatibility.

Online Directories: Utilize online directories to find therapists in your area. Websites like Psychology Today or therapy-specific directories can be useful for browsing profiles and specialties.

Insurance Providers: Check with your insurance provider to identify therapists covered by your plan. This ensures financial feasibility and minimizes out-of-pocket expenses.

Professional Organizations: Explore professional organizations such as the American Psychological Association (APA) for lists of qualified therapists. Membership in such organizations often signifies a commitment to ethical standards and continuing education.

Initial Consultations: Schedule initial consultations with potential therapists to assess their approach, expertise, and whether you feel comfortable working with them. This introductory meeting allows you to ask questions and discuss your specific needs.

Understanding the Therapy Process - What to Expect

Confidentiality: Therapists adhere to strict confidentiality guidelines, creating a safe, open, and honest communication space. They can only breach confidentiality in specific situations, such as if there is a risk of harm to yourself or others.

Collaborative Relationship: Therapy involves a collaborative relationship between the client and therapist. Working together towards defined goals is a key aspect. Your therapist should respect your input and actively involve you in your treatment plan.

Goal Setting: Establish clear goals with your therapist. Whether addressing specific issues or personal growth, setting goals provides direction and helps you track your progress throughout therapy.

Evidence-Based Approaches: Therapists use evidence-based approaches tailored to individual needs. Common modalities include cognitive-behavioral therapy (CBT) or dialectical behavior therapy (DBT). These approaches have been extensively researched and proven effective for various mental health challenges.

Regular Sessions: Therapy typically involves regular sessions, with the frequency determined by individual needs and therapeutic goals. Consistency is essential for achieving lasting results, and your therapist will help you determine the appropriate schedule.

Homework and Reflection: Therapists may assign homework or encourage reflection between sessions to enhance the therapeutic process. These tasks can help you practice and apply the skills and strategies learned in therapy to real-life situations.

Online Mental Health Resources: A Guide for You

Accessing Reliable Mental Health Information

Educational Websites: Explore reputable websites like the National Institute of Mental Health (NIMH) or mental health sections of respected health organizations for reliable information. These websites often provide comprehensive resources on various mental health topics.

University Resources: Check if your college or university offers mental health resources online. Many educational institutions provide information and support services for students, including access to counseling and crisis hotlines.

Online Libraries and Articles: Utilize online libraries and academic articles to access scholarly information related to mental health. Academic databases often provide in-depth insights into the latest research and treatments.

Psychology and Mental Health Apps: Consider using reputable mental health apps that provide information, self-help tools, and resources. Ensure trusted organizations develop these apps, and read user reviews to gauge their effectiveness and user-friendliness. These apps can complement professional treatment and assist in managing mental health challenges.

Online Support Communities

Social Media Groups: Join mental health support groups on social media platforms. These groups provide a space for sharing experiences, seeking advice, and connecting with others facing similar challenges.

Online Forums: Explore dedicated mental health forums and communities where you can anonymously discuss your experiences, offer support, and share coping strategies.

University Forums and Groups:

- Check if your college or university has online forums or groups where students can discuss mental health.
- Share resources.
- Offer support to one another.

Community-Based Platforms: Participate in community-based mental health platforms focusing on specific topics or concerns. These platforms often include expert moderators to ensure a supportive environment.

Teletherapy and Online Counseling

Teletherapy Platforms: Explore teletherapy platforms that connect you with licensed therapists for virtual counseling sessions. Ensure these platforms prioritize user privacy and adhere to ethical standards.

University Counseling Services: Check if your college or university offers online counseling services. Many educational institutions provide virtual counseling sessions to support students' mental health.

Mental Health Hotlines: Access online mental health hotlines that offer immediate support and resources. These services can be crucial during times of crisis or when in need of urgent assistance.

Tailoring Online Mental Health Resources for You

Digital Literacy: Emphasize the importance of digital literacy when navigating online mental health resources. Learn how to evaluate the credibility of information and recognize reputable sources.

Cultural Sensitivity: Highlight the significance of seeking mental health information that is culturally sensitive and inclusive. Explore resources that respect and reflect diverse backgrounds.

Privacy and Security: Emphasize the importance of choosing secure and privacy-focused platforms, especially when engaging in online support communities or teletherapy. Prioritize your privacy for a safe online experience.

Balanced Use: Remember to maintain a balanced use of online mental health resources. While these tools can be valuable, it's essential to complement them with in-person support and professional guidance when needed.

Following this guide can enhance your well-being in the digital age. Emphasizing the importance of cultural sensitivity, digital literacy, and privacy ensures a tailored and holistic approach to your mental health support.

Being There for Friends and Loved Ones

Online Support Communities

Social Media Groups: Join mental health support groups on social media platforms like Facebook or Reddit. These groups provide a space for sharing experiences, seeking advice, and connecting with others facing similar challenges. Remember to be cautious with sharing personal information and choose groups moderated by responsible individuals.

Online Forums: Explore dedicated mental health forums and communities where you can anonymously discuss your experiences, offer support, and share coping strategies. Websites like Reddit have specific subreddits dedicated to mental health discussions, creating a supportive environment for users.

University Forums and Groups: Check if your college or university has online forums or groups where students can discuss mental health. These forums can be valuable for sharing resources, offering support to one another, and finding comfort in knowing that others in your academic community may be going through similar experiences.

Community-Based Platforms: Participate in community-based mental health platforms focusing on specific topics or concerns, such as anxiety, depression, or LGBTQ+ issues. These platforms often include expert moderators to ensure a supportive environment and provide valuable insights from professionals.

Teletherapy and Online Counseling

Teletherapy Platforms: Explore teletherapy platforms that connect you with licensed therapists for virtual counseling sessions. Ensure these platforms prioritize user privacy and adhere to ethical standards. Teletherapy can offer a convenient way to access professional mental health support from the comfort of your home.

University Counseling Services: Check if your college or university offers online counseling services. Many educational institutions provide virtual counseling sessions to support students' mental health. These services are often tailored to the unique challenges that students face.

Mental Health Hotlines: Access online mental health hotlines that offer immediate support and resources. These services can be crucial during times of crisis or when in need of urgent assistance. Examples include crisis text lines or online chat support services.

Tailoring Online Mental Health Resources for You

Digital Literacy: Emphasize the importance of digital literacy when navigating online mental health resources. Learn how to evaluate the credibility of information and recognize reputable sources. Look for websites or resources that cite scientific research and are reviewed by mental health professionals.

Cultural Sensitivity: Highlight the significance of seeking mental health information that is culturally sensitive and inclusive. Explore resources that respect and reflect diverse backgrounds. Culturally competent mental health resources can provide more relevant and effective support.

Privacy and Security: Emphasize the importance of choosing secure and privacy-focused platforms, especially when engaging in online support communities or teletherapy. Prioritize your privacy for a safe online experience by using platforms that encrypt your data and have clear privacy policies.

Balanced Use: Remember to maintain a balanced use of online mental health resources. While these tools can be valuable, it's essential to complement them with in-person support and professional guidance when needed. Online resources can be a supplement to traditional mental health care, not a replacement.

By following this tips, you can enhance your well-being in the digital age. Emphasizing the importance of cultural sensitivity, digital literacy, and privacy ensures a tailored and holistic approach to your mental health support, empowering you to make informed decisions about your well-being.

Being There for Friends and Loved Ones

Providing Emotional Support

Active Listening: Practice active listening when friends or loved ones share their struggles. This involves giving them your full attention, asking open-ended questions, and reflecting on their feelings. Validating their emotions and expressing empathy can make them feel heard and understood.

Avoid Judgment: Refrain from passing judgment or offering unsolicited advice. Creating a non-judgmental space encourages open communication, where individuals feel safe sharing their thoughts and emotions without fear of criticism.

Express Concern: Express genuine concern for their well-being. Let them know you care about their happiness and mental health. Simple gestures like checking in on them regularly or sending a caring message can make a significant difference.

Encourage Openness: Encourage openness about seeking professional help. Normalize the idea that therapy is a positive and proactive step toward better mental health. Share information about available resources and offer to assist them in finding a suitable therapist if needed. Your support can be instrumental in their journey to recovery and well-being.

Key Takeaways

Prioritize Your Mental Health: Mental health is an integral part of overall well-being, influencing your emotions, behaviors, and decisions. Take proactive steps to safeguard your mental health, just as you would with your physical health.

Recognize Signs and Seek Help: Be aware of common mental health challenges like anxiety, depression, and stress-related disorders. If you experience persistent distress, significant behavior changes, or intense emotions that interfere with daily life, consider seeking professional help.

Utilize Online and Offline Resources: Leverage online mental health resources, such as support communities, forums, and teletherapy, for information and support. Maintain a balance between online and offline support, complementing digital resources with in-person connections and professional guidance.

Support Others Compassionately: Learn to provide emotional support to friends and loved ones who may be facing mental health challenges. Practice active listening, express empathy, and encourage open conversations about seeking professional help.

Test Your Knowledge

1. Which of the following is NOT a common symptom of anxiety disorders?

- a. Excessive worry and fear
- b. Rapid heartbeat
- d. Persistent sadness
- d. Muscle tension

2. Depression is often characterized by _____.

- a. Extreme happiness and euphoria
- b. A persistent feeling of sadness and hopelessness
- c. Frequent mood swings
- d. Overly high self-esteem

3. What is one effective way to manage stress and promote mental well-being?

- a. Isolating yourself from others
- b. Avoiding all forms of physical activity
- c. Practicing relaxation techniques like deep breathing and meditation
- d. Consuming large amounts of caffeine

4. A strong support network of friends and family can provide valuable _____ during difficult times.

5. Mental health is just as important as _____ health, and both should be prioritized for overall well-being.

8 MANAGING IMPORTANT DOCUMENTS AND FINANCIAL SECURITY

Importance of Vital Documents:

- Vital documents, such as birth certificates, social security cards, passports, and IDs, are the foundation of your identity and financial stability.

Effective Document Management

- Organized document management offers numerous benefits, including quick responses to life events, financial security, health and emergency preparedness, legal compliance, and reduced stress.

Birth Certificate and Its Significance

- Birth certificates confirm your identity and citizenship in various official transactions.
- It is vital in accessing essential services, proving your citizenship status, and verifying your identity when needed.
- Safeguard it through secure storage, copies with trusted family members, and digital backup.
- Replacement procedures are available if it's lost, involving contacting vital records, verifying your identity, and following government agency instructions.

Social Security Card

- Your Social Security Number (SSN) is essential for various government-related transactions.
- Employers use it for income reporting and payroll, lenders for credit history, and government programs like Social Security, Medicare, and welfare.
- Protect your SSN by minimizing sharing, ensuring data security, and being cautious of scams.
- Replacement procedures are available for lost or stolen SSN cards, which involve reporting the loss to the Social Security Administration, completing an application form, and providing necessary documentation.

Passports and Travel Documents

- Passports are essential for international travel and identification.
- Plan and confirm your eligibility before applying for a passport.
- Gather essential paperwork, including a completed application form, a copy of your birth certificate or previous passport, and a government-issued photo ID.
- Obtain passport-sized photos meeting specified criteria.
- Report and replace lost or stolen passports promptly to your local authorities and the country's consulate or embassy.

Personal Identification Cards

- Understanding the process of obtaining a driver's license or ID is crucial.
- Review eligibility criteria, gather required documents, and prepare for exams if applicable.
- Visit the Department of Motor Vehicles (DMV) to submit your application, provide necessary documentation, and possibly take examinations.
- Ensure you have a valid form of personal identification and know the replacement process if it's lost, including reporting the loss to the police,

visiting the DMV for a replacement, and covering associated fees.

Financial and Legal Paperwork

- Manage income tax documents diligently, understand your insurance policies, and prioritize password security in the digital age.
- Implement secure storage methods for crucial physical and digital documents.
- Regularly review and assess insurance plans to ensure they align with your evolving needs and make adjustments as necessary due to life changes.

Key Takeaways:

Safeguard Vital Documents: Protecting birth certificates, Social Security cards, passports, and IDs is crucial. Safely store physical copies, share copies with trusted family members, and maintain digital backups to ensure you can access essential services and prove your identity when needed.

Stay Informed and Prepared: Understand the processes for obtaining and replacing vital documents, such as birth certificates, Social Security cards, passports, and IDs. Additionally, prioritize secure document management, whether physical or digital, to navigate life's challenges confidently and maintain your financial and personal well-being.

Test Your Knowledge

1. What is the primary purpose of a birth certificate?

- a. To prove your eligibility for government benefits
- b. To confirm your identity and citizenship
- c. To access financial services
- d. To apply for a driver's license

2. What should you do if you lose your Social Security card?

- a. Report it to the local police
- b. Wait for it to turn up on its
- c. Contact the Social Security Admin and follow their replacement process
- d. Use a copy of your birth certificate as a replacement

3. Why is maintaining a digital backup of your passport important?

- a. To easily share it with friends and family
- b. To have a digital souvenir of your travels
- c. To safeguard against theft or loss and facilitate replacement
- d. To expedite passport renewal

AFTERWORD

As we reach the conclusion of "Essential Life Skills for Young Adults," take a moment to reflect on the valuable knowledge you've gained and the practical skills you've developed throughout this book. Our journey together has been dedicated to arming you with the essential life skills you'll need as you transition into adulthood, ready to tackle the diverse challenges and opportunities that await you.

Throughout these chapters, you've delved into a wide array of topics directly relevant to your life as a young adult. From understanding the intricacies of healthcare and wellness to navigating the complex terrain of relationships and sexual health, from mastering the art of social etiquette to becoming financially savvy, and from the intricacies of independent living to the digital landscape, mental health, and the critical aspects of managing essential documents and financial security – you've covered an extensive spectrum of indispensable life skills.

You've learned about the vital importance of health insurance, the keys to fostering healthy and meaningful relationships, the significance of budgeting and prudent money management, and the nuances of online etiquette. You've discovered how to maintain your physical and mental well-being, adapt seamlessly to independent living, and safeguard your essential documents and financial future.

As you conclude this transformative journey, remember that these skills are not mere theoretical concepts but rather practical tools that will serve you exceptionally well in various facets of your life. They are the cornerstones of your future success and overall well-being.

As you continue to progress and face new challenges, embracing opportunities along the way, rest assured that you now possess a solid foundation to navigate the complexities of adulthood. Keep the flames of curiosity and self-improvement burning brightly, continuing to apply these invaluable life skills to enrich not only your own life but also the lives of those around you.

This is not an end, but a fresh beginning, a new chapter in your journey. The knowledge you've acquired here is a potent instrument, and how you wield it will shape your future. Therefore, with unwavering confidence, resilience, and an unwavering commitment to seizing every opportunity that comes your way, step boldly into the next exciting phase of your life.

Congratulations on successfully completing this journey! Your future is luminous, and you are exceptionally well-prepared to meet it head-on with confidence and competence. Continue to flourish, persevere, and evolve into the best version of yourself. The world is yours to conquer, and you are more than ready for the challenge!

A SHINING OPPORTUNITY TO HELP ANOTHER YOUNG ADULT LIKE YOU!

WANT TO HELP OTHERS?

You've made it through the book, and I'm stoked you decided to dive into this journey with me. Now that you've soaked up all the essential life skills I've packed in here, I'm inviting you to join the crew of folks who are putting this knowledge into action.

As you've flipped through these pages and picked up wisdom along the way, think about how these skills can play out in your life. If this book hit the mark for you or sparked some aha moments, I'd seriously appreciate it if you dropped a review. Sharing your take can clue others in on how these insights might light up their path too.

No rush, though! Whenever you're feeling inspired, let me know how things are going. Your thoughts are super valuable, not just to me but to others riding this wave of adulting.

Thanks for rolling with me on this ride of personal growth and empowerment. I'm all ears for your stories and insights, ready to hear how you're making these pages come to life in your world!

ANSWER KEY

Chapter 1 :

Why is it important to have health insurance if you can?

Correct Answer: To protect yourself from high medical costs

Why are wellness visits and preventive care important?

Correct Answer: They detect and prevent health issues early

How can getting an estimate of cost help you?

Correct Answer: It allows you to plan your budget and make informed decisions

How can you help keep your oral care healthy?

Correct Answer: All of the above.

What is the difference between in and out-of-network?

Correct Answer: In-network providers have agreements with your insurance company, while out-of-network providers do not

A fixed amount you pay for a service is called what?

Correct Answer: Co-pay

Chapter 2:

What is an essential aspect of cultivating healthy romantic relationships?

Correct Answer: Open and honest communication

Why is it crucial to practice safe dating on dates?

Correct Answer: To ensure your safety

What is an integral part of understanding sexual health?

Correct Answer: All of the above

Which of the following is an example of an unhealthy romantic relationship?

Correct Answer: Emotional abuse and control

What does consent mean in the context of sexual activity?

Correct Answer: It encompasses clear communication, mutual agreement, and willingness from all parties involved.

Chapter 3:

What is one key purpose of etiquette in various scenarios?

Correct Answer: Demonstrating respect and consideration

When attending a wedding, what are the proper etiquette guidelines to follow?

Correct Answer: Bring a gift even if you can't attend

Why is tipping for dining, deliveries, and personal care important in various cultures and industries?

Correct Answer: All of the above

What should you do when meeting someone's parents for the first time?

Correct Answer: All of the above.

How can you express gratitude to service providers who offer exceptional service in the digital realm?

Correct Answer: Provide virtual tips or positive feedback

Chapter 4:

What is the primary purpose of creating a personal budget?

Correct Answer: To manage your income and expenses

Why is it important to make on-time payments for your credit card bills?

Correct Answer: Because it helps build and maintain a positive credit history

What is the significance of an emergency fund?

Correct Answer: It provides a financial safety net for unexpected expenses

Which of the following is NOT a factor that affects your credit score?

Correct Answer: Your favorite color

What is the recommended credit utilization ratio for maintaining a positive credit score?

Correct Answer: Below 30%

Which of the following is NOT a step in balancing your checkbook?

Correct Answer: Avoiding checking your bank statements

Which of the following is NOT a strategy for managing debt?

Correct Answer: Accumulating new debt regularly

Chapter 5:

When budgeting for rent, it's recommended not to spend more than what percentage of your monthly income?

Correct Answer: 30%

What should you consider when choosing an apartment location?

Correct Answer: All of the above (The question implies multiple considerations are important, including proximity to work or school, noise level, etc.)

Before signing a lease agreement, it's essential to carefully read and understand all the _____ to avoid any surprises later.

Correct Answer: Terms and conditions (or clauses)

Regular decluttering and creating a cleaning schedule helps in maintaining a _____ living space.

Correct Answer: Organized and clean (or tidy)

True or False: Emergency preparedness includes having a well-equipped emergency kit with essentials like non-perishable food and water.

Correct Answer: True

Chapter 6:

What does HTTPS in a website URL indicate?

Correct Answer: Highly Secure Encryption Protocol

Which of the following is NOT a recommended practice for online privacy?

Correct Answer: Conducting sensitive transactions on public Wi-Fi networks

What is the purpose of Two-Factor Authentication (2FA)?

Correct Answer: It adds an extra layer of security by requiring a second form of verification.

When meeting sellers or buyers in person for transactions, it's important to choose _____, well-lit, and public locations.

Correct Answer: Safe (or secure)

Leaving constructive feedback after an online transaction can help others make informed decisions. (True/False)

Correct Answer: True

Chapter 7:

Which of the following is NOT a common symptom of anxiety disorders?

Correct Answer: Persistent sadness

Depression is often characterized by _____.

Correct Answer: A persistent feeling of sadness and hopelessness

What is one effective way to manage stress and promote mental well-being?

Correct Answer: Practicing relaxation techniques like deep breathing and meditation

A strong support network of friends and family can provide valuable _____ during difficult times.

Correct Answer: Emotional support (or support)

Mental health is just as important as _____ health, and both should be prioritized for overall well-being.

Correct Answer: Physical

Chapter 8:

What is the primary purpose of a birth certificate?

Correct Answer: To confirm your identity and citizenship

What should you do if you lose your Social Security card?

Correct Answer: Contact the Social Security Administration and follow their replacement process

Why is maintaining a digital backup of your passport important?

Correct Answer: To safeguard against theft or loss and facilitate replacement

BIBLIOGRAPHY

- ARRICCA ELIN SANSONE, EMY RODRIGUEZ FLORES. (2019, Dec 20). *50+ Little Social Etiquette Rules Everyone Should Follow.* Retrieved from Country Living: https://www.countryliving.com/life/g15915245/social-etiquette/

- Armenia, U. (2022, April 25). *Dispelling Myths and Misconceptions About Vaccines.* Retrieved from UNICEF Armenia: https://www.unicef.org/armenia/en/stories/dispelling-myths-and-misconceptions-about-vaccines

- BLOG, F. (2021, Feb 01). *Car Safety Tips EVERY College Student Should Know.* Retrieved from Feed that Nation: https://feedthatnation.com/car-safety-tips-every-college-student-should-know/

- Cambria. (2023, February 22). *The Importance of Financial Literacy for College Students.* Retrieved from Cambria: https://cambriaschool.com/blog/the-importance-of-financial-literacy-for-college-students/

- Christine Frank, D. (2019, March 8). *Everything You Need to Know About Dental and Oral Health.* Retrieved from Healthline: https://www.healthline.com/health/dental-and-oral-health#_noHeaderPrefixedContent

- Egan, J. (2023, Nov 7). *How to Balance a Checkbook.* Retrieved from U.S.News: https://www.usnews.com/banking/articles/how-to-balance-a-checkbook

- Elizabeth Davis, RN . (2023, Dec 17). *HMO, PPO, EPO, POS—Which Plan Should You Choose?* Retrieved from VeryWell health:

https://www.verywellhealth.com/hmo-ppo-epo-pos-whats-the-difference-1738615

- Filaski, C. (2022, April 26). *7 things to know when cooking as a college student*. Retrieved from Cougarbuzz: https://cougarbuzz.com/2022/04/26/7-things-to-know-when-cooking-as-a-college-student/

- Hopkins, J. (n.d.). *Medication Management and Safety Tips*. Retrieved from Johns Hopkins: https://www.hopkinsmedicine.org/health/wellness-and-prevention/help-for-managing-multiple-medications

- Jensen, M. (2023, Oct 3). *How to Schedule Appointments With Your Patients? 12 Proven Strategies*. Retrieved from DemandHub: https://www.demandhub.co/articles/patient-appointment-scheduling/

- Kovacs, K. (2022, Nov 23). *Understanding Sexual Health in College*. Retrieved from Best Colleges: https://www.bestcolleges.com/resources/sexual-health/

- M, A. K. (n.d.). *What are the most effective ways to teach digital literacy and online safety?* Retrieved from LinkedIn: https://www.linkedin.com/advice/0/what-most-effective-ways-teach-digital-literacy

- Maheshwari, R. (2023, Dec 27). *What Is Health Insurance: Meaning, Benefits & Types*. Retrieved from forbes: https://www.forbes.com/advisor/in/health-insurance/what-is-health-insurance/

- Meyers, J. (2022, April 01). *10 tips to help you find the perfect apartment after college*. Retrieved from CNBC: https://www.cnbc.com/2022/04/01/10-tips-to-help-you-find-the-perfect-apartment-after-college.html

- RAINN. (n.d.). *Online Dating and Dating App Safety Tips*. Retrieved from RAINN: https://www.rainn.org/articles/online-dating-and-dating-app-safety-tips

- Ramsey. (2023, Dec 8). *How to Organize Your Important Documents*. Retrieved from RAMSEY: https://www.ramseysolutions.com/retirement/organizing-your-important-documents

- Ravenscraft, E. (2020, Jan 23). *An Adult's Guide to Social Skills, for Those Who Were Never Taught*. Retrieved from The New York Times: https://www.nytimes.com/2020/01/23/smarter-living/adults-guide-to-social-skills.html

- Team, A. A. (2022, April 12). *Digital Literacy in 2023*. Retrieved from Academy: https://www.avast.com/c-digital-literacy

- Vadnal, J. (2023, February 2). *The Ultimate Guide to Tipping Etiquette in Every Situation—and When Not to Tip*. Retrieved from Real Simple: https://www.realsimple.com/work-life/money/money-etiquette/tipping-etiquette-guide

- Vaghefi, S. (2023, May 09). *Etiquette Definition, Types & Rules*. Retrieved from Study.com : https://study.com/academy/lesson/etiquette-definition-types-rules.html

- WPShealth. (n.d.). *Health Insurance Terminology and Definitions*. Retrieved from WPShealth: https://www.wpshealth.com/resources/customer-resources/health-insurance-terminology.shtml

- Young, E. (2022, Jul 15). *Mental Health in College: Why It's Important and What You Can Do*. Retrieved from Admisions.usf: https://admissions.usf.edu/blog/mental-health-in-college-why-its-important-and-what-you-can-do

- Zubair, M. (2023, Oct 29). *The Importance of Financial Literacy for Young Adults*. Retrieved from Medium: https://medium.-

com/@MuhammadZubairMalik/the-importance-of-financial-literacy-for-young-adults-21d34a011339

Made in the USA
Las Vegas, NV
04 May 2024

89508762R20215